A Small-Town GIRL

DIANA ANYANGO

Diana Anyango

First Published in Great Britain in 2022 by

LOVE AFRICA PRESS

103 Reaver House, 12 East Street, Epsom KT17 1HX

www.loveafricapress.com

LOVE AFRICA
PRESS
African Love Stories

Also available in paperback format

BLURB

Lucy Akinyi returns home to lick her wounds after a bad break-up and finds purpose in advocating for children's rights. But the hurt has left her slow to trust and almost numb to love.

Adams Okal goes into the heart of Kachieng' to set up his dream ranch and have some peace, away from deception, war, and despair. But without the army, he feels like a blind man groping in the dark and starts to feel lonely without his family until he meets Lucy.

Their physical attraction makes him want her. Yet, Adams can't settle for a brief liaison. Lucy pulls his heartstrings like no other. However, she is resistant to getting entangled with a man in uniform. Are they strong enough to demolish all the barriers and discover love on the other side?

This book mentions child abuse, sexual assault, gender-based violence, PTSD and suicide.

DEDICATION

To all the strong women loving their men in uniform.

ACKNOWLEDGEMENTS

All glory belongs to God for planting this story in me.

Dearest reader, thank you very much for choosing this book. Adams and Akinyi await to sail you through their love story.

I never thought I'll say this, but here we go. Thank you, Paul Victor, for providing inspiration for this story.

Kiru Taye, thank you very much for taking a chance on this story. Keep on lighting this African romance path. It's high time we celebrate African love and happily ever after.

CHAPTER ONE

The pride of a woman is to get married.

Lucy Akinyi mulled over her grandma's favourite statement as she plopped on her seat, fatigued after finishing her share of the morning chores.

"My daughter, it is three months in this hell hole. You should get back to Nairobi. There aren't any opportunities for you in this town. You are wasting your time here," her mother, Nyakisumo, walked into the house with an aluminium tea kettle in hand. She placed it on the table and sat down, the seat squeaking under her heavy weight.

Akinyi groaned inwards, dreading and hating this conversation in equal measure. It was like this every morning. Was home no longer a haven?

She'd returned home after everything in her life had fallen apart. David ended their six-year relationship on the day she thought he would finally propose to her. Pain radiated in her chest when she remembered the break-up.

Afterwards came the tragedy with Kadogo, and then Akinyi was sacked from her job. Misery came in pairs, indeed.

Hence, she'd escaped to her hometown to lick her wounds and patch her life together.

Breaking out of her trance, she found her mother glaring at her.

"Mother, don't even start. I am not leaving. I know that my aunts have filled up your head with nonsense. I will get married, eventually. Don't worry so much about me," she countered.

Her mother and grandma had been hinting that she ought to find a man and get on with having babies. According to them, a woman's office is in the husband's kitchen. No matter how learned or successful a woman became in life, it was useless if she wasn't married.

However, she wanted both a career and a loving marriage. As her thirtieth birthday approached, Akinyi understood her mother's worries. Most graduates stayed in cities with plenty of opportunities. Then, after a few years, they returned, driving big cars and building mansions. Most of Akinyi's local agemates were already married, with two or more children.

Nyakisumo was worried that she won't get married since the town didn't have eligible bachelors. The few good men doing meaningful work were primary and secondary school teachers. Furthermore, the natives of Rachuonyo couldn't intermarry since Rachuonyo were believed to be related. Hence it was taboo.

Most of the young men in the area were elementary school dropouts. They spent all their time and meagre income on bhang, locally brewed busaa and chang'aa. They wreaked havoc, stealing property and livestock, spending the better part of the days at the Agawo centre playing simbi and plotting the night raids. They'd even renamed the place Agawo si Kenya.

As if to buttress her mother's fears, outside the window, Daddy, one of the Agawo si Kenya lot, staggered past, singing loudly, drunkenly. "Achienge, Achi Bella ooh you make... very sweet syrup and moisturising aka chwakramyacin."

Akinyi caught a glimpse of despair in Nyakisumo's gaze as she shook her head and walked out of the house.

***

One of Akinyi's young cousins of about twenty years was being married off. The husband had brought six heads of cow, and it was the talk of the small town.

"My daughter, what are your plans for marriage? The young ones are leaving, but I have never seen you or heard gossip about your engagement with any man," Nyakisumo asked, looking at the faraway hills.

Akinyi giggled before asking, "Do you have people spying on me?"

"Not really, but you know if something like that were to happen, it wouldn't escape the watchful eyes and sharp ears of the people." Mother chuckled.

"Mama, I haven't found anybody whom I love enough to want to settle down with. I want a prince charming that will sweep me off my feet, and we would live happily ever after," she said, her eyes gaining a dreamy look.

Her mother pinched her on the cheek, bringing her back to reality.

"What, Mama? Can't a girl have dreams?"

"Some dreams are just impossible. You are talking about the kind of love found in romance novels and soap operas. It isn't real, so wake up." The woman waved her off, a frown rumpling her face.

"Thank you, Mama. It is a beautiful dream, and I'll keep holding onto it." Akinyi sighed.

"Your father and I weren't full of passion or the wild love you talk about. We were introduced to each other by your uncle, Oluoch." She grinned, the fond memory lighting up her face. "The first time I set my eyes on him, I knew that I had found the one, and I was right. We were different in the beginning, but as the years went by, we fell into a rhythm of our own."

"You must miss him very much, don't you?"

"I do, with every passing heartbeat. He was a responsible man and always made sure that we ate well and had a roof over our heads. I found myself loving him as time passed. He was my friend, companion, and the love of my life." Nyakisumo rubbed her hands up and down her arm as if the memory left coldness in its wake.

Akinyi could only visualize her father sitting under the mango tree with her mother. They had rarely talked. Her father had been a man of few words, but their silences had never been awkward. On the contrary, it had been full of peace and tranquillity that no conversation could suffice. People who didn't know each other felt the need to blabber away to avoid a lull in the discussion, not them.

"But I find it funny that I never even once saw you hold hands or kiss," Akinyi said.

Her mother smiled, exposing her mbanya, the gap between her two front teeth.

"Like I said, our love wasn't that wild. It wasn't expressive in that way. He did his part, and I did mine with the housework like cooking for him, washing his clothes. For us, that was always enough."

"It sounds so boring to me, I swear. I want someone spontaneous. Someone who can surprise me with flowers, hold my hand and go for evening walks," she gushed.

Her mother gave her a faraway look before saying, "Then I bet I won't be seeing my grandchildren soon. The men you have described are rare species if at all they exist, especially in these parts."

"Mama, don't worry so much about that. I will find that man, and you will have many grandchildren who can make up a football team. Just wait and see," Akinyi babbled, and her mother laughed.

Nyakisumo sometimes mentioned how lucky she'd been to have Akinyi. She classed her daughter as one of the best things that ever happened in her

life, and she would have never traded her for a son
either.

Akinyi's smile wavered as her mind wandered to
David.

He hadn't called for four months now. This was
unlike him. Was he serious about ending things
between them? Had he moved on without her?

Her mind flashed to that hot afternoon he had
told her he wanted out. It had been her twenty-
ninth birthday party. She had invited close friends
to her house in Kahawa Sukari to celebrate. David
had strutted in with his friends, looking tall and
handsome as always, his jeans snuggling to those
thick thighs, his white t-shirt moulding to his broad
chest. Her very own man in uniform, with the army
hair cut to match. His chocolate brown skin
glowing. Every time he had smiled at her, her heart
raced. She had been ready to be his wife.

He'd kept pushing up their engagement because
he'd claimed that he wanted to pay fees first for his
siblings. Orphaned when they were young, the
responsibility rested squarely on him. Akinyi had
understood and waited. But, six years down the
line, he hadn't yet popped the question. His
brothers had finished school, and she'd hoped that
he would finally move things along.

When the last guest had left, he closed the
distance between them, his eyes trained on her. Her
breath caught. This is the day.

"There's something I want to tell you." He took
her hand and led her to the couch.

Once seated, he played with the button to her
dress, regarding her closely.

"What is it, David?" she asked, nerves coiling at the pit of her stomach. Nobody would surely break your heart on your birthday, right?

"I can't go on with this relationship. I am sorry." He deadpanned, leaning back on his seat.

Laughing shakily, she scooted close to him. "You're kidding, right?"

He shook his head. "No, Akinyi. We're different. I want different."

She didn't understand his vague statement, and she pushed him to expound.

"You are tough headed. You can't be a submissive wife. You are too independent." His lips spewed words that hurt her to her core, breaking her heart into tiny pieces and trampling on it.

She covered her ears with her hands, migraine setting in. Six years, and all for what?

She remembered closing the door behind him and the tears she had been trying to hold onto washing her face. The memories of the rest of that day were blurry at best, Ephy consoling her, trying to make sense of everything.

CHAPTER TWO

Akinyi and Adhiambo boarded a matatu that only had two passengers after shopping for food at Oyugis Market.

Outside the waiting minibus waiting to fill up, traders haggled with their customers in loud voices. The place bustled with activity, the crowd milling, cars and boda-bodas honking with impatient drivers and motorists. Eventually, the vehicle was packed with passengers, even given sambaza, and they set off.

She alighted with her friend at the Bongu stage, and they began their walk home on the dusty murram road. The hot afternoon sun made their clothes stick to their bodies.

"Akinyi, have you heard of the young man who has just landed in the village with a Prado?" Adhiambo asked, wiggling her eyebrows.

Akinyi smiled and wondered if there was any news that escaped her friend's inquisitive ears. She was meant to be a newscaster.

"No. What about him?" Akinyi asked.

"I have never seen such a handsome man in my whole life. But that is maybe because I have never

13

gone beyond the Nyanza region. But still, he is a rare kind. Imagine me at my age standing by the roadside admiring a man." Adhiambo grinned like a bewitched woman, making Akinyi laugh. Her friend continued her tale. "The area girls are parading at his compound in the hope of ensnaring him. Maybe we should join them, or we will die old spinsters. Yesterday my younger sister called my mother, explaining her plans to bring her husband. Can you imagine that?"

Anxiety marring her face before she mimicked her grandmother's high-pitched voice. "If by next year you don't get married, my granddaughter, you may never get a husband because your beauty is fading."

They burst into laughter, high-fiving each other.

"You are just 24 years old, yet you are complaining. What should I do then? Wail? Marriage is here to stay. Don't rush just because you are pressured. Do it at your own pace," Akinyi said for the umpteenth time.

Everyone seemed keen on dropping hints about her biological clock ticking at twenty-nine years old, but she wasn't shaken. She had her plans, and right now, marriage was not a priority, not after what David did to her. It was slowly dawning on her that David had been serious about ending things. He still hadn't called, and he didn't pick up her calls when she called him.

She felt very empty inside. So used to his late-night calls, now she tossed and turned, staring at her phone expectantly. It was like she was a walking cocoon. She had come home to lick her wounds by working her ass off and forgetting everything. But she had been telling herself a lie. Finally, the truth had caught up with her at lightning speed.

She could not just forget everything and pretend it never happened. It had. But it was still very painful, very raw. She did not know what would assuage the pain, the hurt.

Akinyi was still lost in her thoughts when Adhiambo pinched her back to the present.

"That's his car approaching," she said gleefully. When Akinyi stared at her in confusion, she said impatiently, stomping her feet on the ground, "The new guy I just told you about."

They turned in the direction of the approaching sleek, black car.

Adhiambo waved ceaselessly at it, smiling broadly.

Akinyi suppressed the urge to slap her hard across the face. The man would think they were some naïve girls who had never seen a handsome man behind the wheels.

She retreated as the car halted beside them, and the window rolled down. She froze, her feet rooted to the ground.

Adhiambo had been right about the man being handsome, but handsome did not even begin to describe him.

He was bald, had a strong jawline, and sported a beard. For some reason, Akinyi loved it because it gave him a dangerous appearance. His smoky-brown eyes stared at her in unabashed admiration.

15

His mouth curved into a grin, making her stomach churn.

She quickly licked her suddenly dry lips and looked away.

"Hello, ladies. Can I give you a lift?" he asked, getting out of the car.

"That would be lovely. Thanks," Adhiambo quickly answered, already jumping into the backseat.

Akinyi stood her ground as she looked at the man in his full glory. He was very tall, over six feet if she wasn't wrong, his skin chocolate-dark. And the body. Ooh, my God. Nobody had the right to look that good—the broad chest, muscular arms, and thick thighs.

Her knees weakened as her pulse pounded in her ears.

"Akinyi, let's go!" Adhiambo called impatiently, throwing her hands up in the air.

"No. I don't board strangers' cars. Maybe he will kidnap us," Akinyi spoke while gazing straight into the aforementioned stranger's sexy eyes.

The man grinned, shaking his head as his hot gaze scalded her body. Nothing subtle about his ogling, as if he didn't want her to have any doubt about his intention.

Her toes curled in her shoes as she tried to act calm and nonchalant.

"Come on. I am not a kidnapper," he said hoarsely.

"We cannot be so sure about that, can we? What's your name?" she asked.

Adhiambo rolled her eyes. "Akinyi!"

Akinyi ignored her, folding her arms across her chest.

"I am Adams Okal. I am building my ranch just next to Achego Catholic church. What's your name?" he asked, leaning his hip against the vehicle and crossing his ankles.

"If you have ears, I believe you have heard my friend mention my name. Furthermore, I am harmless. I can't kidnap you even if I had that in mind." Akinyi looked him over, from his brown safari boots, the thigh-hugging jeans, through to his fitted blue shirt.

Finally, her gaze landed on his, and she winked. His eyes widened in surprise.

Akinyi climbed into the open car, and he closed the door for her, the corner of his mouth turning up in a mysterious smile. He was a gentleman too. What was not to love about this man? There was a companionable silence as he drove along the dusty untarred road. He dropped Adhiambo at her doorstep, and she bade them goodbye.

Akinyi hesitated briefly, wanting to get out and walk the rest of the way. Was she scared of being alone with the man? Silence ensued as they continued with the journey.

She stared at his hands on the steering wheel. He held it with an effortless grace like he was caressing it. His long finger had her mind racing with hot sex scenes. She quickly lifted her gaze to the rear-view mirror and caught him staring at her. Was he doing the steering thing intentionally? She felt both hot and cold at once. She averted her gaze to the window and saw the familiar gate to her home right ahead of her. Relief washed over her.

"Pull over, please," she said in a near whisper.

He stopped the car and rushed out to open the door for her. She jumped out of the car and shook his outstretched hand. It was rough, warm, and inviting. She pulled hers away from his and walked home hurriedly.

A glance over her shoulder showed him leaning on his car, watching her. Her cheeks heated as she entered the compound. She heard the revving of the car engine as it sped away.

Akinyi whispered a simple prayer when she reached the house without stumbling. The man stirred something deep inside her, which she didn't want to explore.

She still wasn't over David and hoped he would call, pleading for forgiveness. She had to leave the door open for him, in case, didn't she? They'd been through so much in their six years together, and she didn't want to throw it all away.

Even as she thought it, she hated herself.

You're wasting your time waiting for David, a little voice whispered inside her.

Still, she glanced at the phone, hoping it would ring.

CHAPTER THREE

Adams switched on the radio, and Ferre Gola's hauntingly beautiful baritone filled the room with his Pakadjuma song. Leaning into his seat, nodding to the beats, his mind wandered to Akinyi.

He was accustomed to always getting what he wanted, and he wanted Akinyi.

Had done from the first time he'd seen her with her friend. The women were stunning.

Adhiambo was short, with a light-brown skin tone and curves in all the right places. But he didn't feel any attraction towards her.

Akinyi was something else, their chemistry bubbling close to the surface. He could not get his mind off their first meeting. The big eyes that had winked at him made him chuckle. What had the woman been thinking? The gap between her two upper teeth, mbanya, a symbol of true African beauty, had wooed him. Her smooth, brown skin, as rich and lustrous as the Kachieng soil, beckoned him to run his fingers over her.

He recalled her asking whether he was a kidnapper and chuckled.

More like woman-napping her because nothing about her body was kidlike. She had full breasts that strained against her purple dress. How would they feel in his hands? Were her buttocks big under her skater dress which didn't do them justice? He visualized undressing her to confirm his suspicion. Imagined plunging into her sumptuous lips, kissing her until they were both out of breath.

The woman tempted him in every way without even trying hard. Maybe she was his Eve, and he did not mind getting seduced by her.

He hadn't come to this town looking for love. Or was it lust? He had come to build his dream ranch and have some peace of mind. The war had been cruel. The fifteen years he had dedicated to the army had made him and destroyed him.

It made him because he had money, loads of money. Plus, he had businesses that generated millions of shillings every year. Still, at 35 years old, he didn't have someone to share it all with.

His fiancée had left him eight years ago when he had gone for Linda Inchi's operation at the Somali border. He didn't hold it against her. He had been gone for weeks on end. Sometimes even for six months continuous. The frontline had been in remote places and trying to contact each other had been a nightmare. They had drifted apart. Their untended garden of love had become overgrown with long weeds. He hadn't been able to give her the dedication she had needed. The last he heard of her was that she was still single.

Now, he wanted a fresh start. However, did he have what it took to commit to a woman?

After his break-up, he had not bothered with a stable relationship. Of course, he had a string of women to quench his sexual desires every now and then. But that was getting so old and boring. Casual sex and one-night stands only fulfilled his physical needs.

Still, his thoughts wandered off to Linda, his mistress. He had only gone there twice since he retired. The aching need in his loins reminded him that seeing her again wasn't such a bad idea. He planned to end their deal, but he could not just quit. He was going to do so slowly.

Akinyi's face flashed in his mind. The woman intrigued him. He was willing to end the thing with Linda just so he could explore Akinyi. No doubt.

***

Adams lit his cigarette as he sat on the front porch. As the nicotine filled his lungs, he looked at the bright crescent moon, illuminating the darkness he felt deep in his soul. The fumes filled the void creeping onto him.

The ranch was too quiet and lonely. His mind roamed these days, flipping through the past, wrapping him in pain.

He remembered his mother and the day he'd told her that he'd enlisted in the army. At the time, her face had streaked with tears, and he'd wondered whether they were tears of joy or sorrow.

Now, he knew better. They had been tears of deep sorrow.

She'd known how the army changed men into beasts and unfeeling beings. She'd known it first-hand since her father had been in the military.

Suffering from post-war trauma and haunted by the battlefields' ghosts, he'd blown his brains out to escape his torturous life. He'd left Adam's grandmother a young widow and his mother, a fatherless child.

According to his mother, the military meant pain, sorrow, and death, but that hadn't stopped Adams from pursuing his lifelong dream. He'd wanted to find out for himself and not let others' experiences determine his destiny.

"My son, take care. May God Almighty protect you," she had told him before he'd left home.

Tears had stung his eyes, but he hadn't shed any. He hadn't known that would be the last time he would see her alive.

Now, he was tortured because he hadn't been there to hold her hands when she took her last breath. He'd been away defending his country—a noble cause, they said. What about her mother, who was supporting her? The army hadn't cared. His commander had informed him that they were in the middle of a delicate operation. Therefore, he couldn't just up and leave.

When he'd been finally granted the chance to go home, his mother had already been buried.

The feeling of emptiness, loneliness, and sadness engulfed him as he'd looked at the cold grave. He'd wondered how life could be short, here today and gone tomorrow. It had felt so unreal.

The pained look on his father's face had mirrored his own. Papa had always loved his mother profoundly and to lose her was to lose himself. He didn't speak much, but the cold accusation on his eyes never eluded Adams. It was like he was blaming Adams for something. What? He didn't know.

His brother, Seth, eventually confirmed his worst fears. "I hope now you are happy. You sent Mama to an early grave."

"What are you talking about?" Adams had demanded.

"After you left, she would sit for long hours staring into space. She was always afraid of receiving phone calls for fear that they were calling to report your death. It soon developed into depression, and no matter what the doctors did, she only deteriorated."

"No way, you are lying," he'd countered, not wanting to believe any of it.

"It's the truth, you selfish son of a gun. Now you can go back to slaughtering people. You should know one thing for sure. For as long as I live, I will never forgive you," his brother had sworn.

Adams' heart had sunken to his stomach, and he'd angrily stormed out of their home, going to Kisumu. He'd visited Linda that night, kissing her hard and having rough sex with her. Afterwards, he'd apologized to her for being harsh, but she didn't begrudge him. Instead, she'd held him close to her heart as he'd cried and caressed his back, whispering comforting words.

He had woken up early the next day with the dark cloud hanging over him. Too embarrassed to let Linda see him, he'd travelled back to Somalia, never returning home. During his leave, he always went to the apartment he had rented out for Linda.

They'd spent the entire month making love, sleeping, eating out and making love again. Their love life wasn't complicated. Linda always knew what he wanted and never asked for more. It was just the kind of relationship that suited him, no strings attached.

Despite being away from home, he still missed his family. It felt good to belong, have roots, and have a safe place to return to when the world got rough.

Sometimes he wondered how his father was fairing. Had he remarried? He doubted if his father could love another woman. Or perhaps he just didn't want to believe that his father could marry someone else.

Papa had taught him numerous things about being a man and the ways of their people—looking after livestock, respecting the elderly and loving women.

What would his old man think of his life now? He would be disappointed about his arrangement with Linda, that was for sure.

Adams remembered his siblings. Seth was older than him by three years. They had been close growing up. Seth had taught him how to swim in the rivers and to hunt.

However, he missed his sister, Val, the most. She'd been born when he'd been twelve years old, and he'd loved carrying her on his back despite Seth ridiculing him. Adams had always wanted to protect her from the big scary world. When he'd left to join the army, she had been only eight years old. Now, she was twenty. Aside from his mother, she was the second woman he'd cared for more than his own life. He wondered how she'd turned out. Had she gone to college? Was she married?

So many questions and few answers. So many years had gone by since he left home. Too much time had passed.

Did they still blame him for the death of his mother?

Sometimes he was tempted to drive home and get all these answers. But something held him back. He didn't know whether it was fear or pride. Or a little bit of both.

CHAPTER FOUR

Akinyi headed to the Abururu spring with Adhiambo, carrying 20-litre yellow jerricans in hand. The January morning sun warmed them as dewy grass wetted their feet. A new gossip swept the small town of Oyugis, and Akinyi's return had been pushed aside to allow for this news.

"Have you heard what Ocholla has done?" Adhiambo rushed to say, swinging her can as if trying to temper down the urge to share the latest village gist.

Akinyi had no idea what she was talking about since she spent most of her time at home. However, her friend took after her mother and had a thirst for gossip, ensuring that news reached all corners of the small town.

"No. What has he done this time?" Akinyi asked, reluctant to join in the gossip but also intrigued.

Ocholla was always in the limelight for all the wrong reasons. He was a thin, short man known for ido witchcraft. He had inherited the skill from his mother, who was rumoured to bewitch young children and adults while eating food.

However, Ocholla performed his act at night, running naked when the urge became too strong. Some people even said he would grow big and round like a pumpkin if he didn't give in to the desire. He constantly disturbed people's peace at night, kicking at their doors and pouring sand through their roofs' ventilation. But the locals were used to all this. It was no longer news.

"Ocholla has impregnated Awino, the daughter of Okumu," Adhiambo said in a low voice.

Akinyi shook her head, not believing her ears. Ocholla was in his late sixties. How could he defile a girl old enough to be his granddaughter?

"Awino's mother has reported the matter to the chief, right?" she asked as they reached Abururu springs, the water bubbling as it flowed away.

"Are you out of your mind? She cannot do that. Everybody fears Ocholla and his rogue sons," her friend explained, filling her can.

Awino's mother was a widow with five young children. She didn't have the money or the resources to pursue justice for her daughter. Moreover, in Oyugis, people were good neighbours. Good neighbourliness demanded that she not report the matter to the chief, keep it low and solve it amongst themselves.

Akinyi was astounded that such a backward way of thinking still existed here. "But Awino is only thirteen years old. I understand that Awino's mother is helpless. What are the rest of the locals doing about it?"

They started the long walk home.

Her friend turned quickly to look at her with an incredulous expression, almost dropping the full jerrican well-balanced on her head in the process. "Don't be ridiculous! If you have not noticed, everyone minds their business in this town, and I suggest you do the same."

As they resumed walking, outrage filled Akinyi. She'd always felt the locals were one and cared about one another, but that was a long time ago. She'd been away for so long, and so much had changed. Now, instead of helping, all people did was talk about it in hushed tones, sweeping it under the carpet, maintaining peace. But what peace?

Awino was a child whose bright future had been shattered by Ocholla. Only in Class Six at Agawo Primary School, her innocence had been stolen. Yet people behaved like it was no big deal and her mother was too helpless to do anything.

Akinyi wouldn't keep quiet, though. She would fight for Awino with all she had. Images of Kadogo's hollow eyes flashed before her. This was one horror and regret that she would carry to her grave. But, at least by helping out Awino, her troubled soul would be freed, even if partly.

CHAPTER FIVE

When Akinyi got home, her mother was in the kitchen, preparing ugali on the three stones fireplace, smoke making her eyes water.

"Mother, have you heard that Ocholla has impregnated Awino?" she asked, sitting on a three-legged stool.

"Of course. Word travels fast around here. That man did a heinous act to the poor little girl, and he wants to marry her," her mother said, shaping the ugali with a cooking stick and letting it simmer.

What had become of this town? Ocholla needed to be behind bars for defiling a minor. Once charged, he would spend a good part of his old age in prison. Yet, people wanted to sweep the act under the carpet and crown Ocholla with a second wife.

"I will ensure that man pays for his horrible crime." In anger, Akinyi pushed off the stool like it had gotten too hot, and it fell backwards.

"Akinyi! Let Awino be. She is not the first girl to be defiled. She has her people to fight for her," the older woman pleaded in a concerned tone, obviously hoping to dissuade her daughter from taking up what seemed like a deadly cause. "Didn't I tell you about the chief of a neighbouring town who was slaughtered like a chicken while trying to settle a dispute? I don't want anything to happen to you."

"Mother, it won't come to that," she replied defiantly. As her parent always commented, Akinyi had taken up her father's stubbornness. Once the fire was lit inside her and she made up her mind to do something, there was no stopping her.

"Ah, this child will be the death of me."

Her mother's lamentation as she headed out again didn't deter her. She was not going to sit around just like everyone else. The last time she took her sweet time, Kadogo hanged herself, leaving her a suicide note. She could not fail another person if she could help it.

The sight of Awino's home—a small, almost-collapsing, grass-thatched house—made Akinyi more determined to do the right thing. Three of Awino's siblings played outside, barefooted and in tattered clothes. They informed Akinyi that their mother and Awino were on the farm.

Since it was the harvesting season, most folks were busy harvesting maize. Nevertheless, the tallest of the trio went to call them from the shamba. He walked with his head cast down and his hand crisscrossed to hide the holes on his brown pair of shorts, exposing his bare buttocks.

When Awino's mother arrived, she stared at Akinyi as if wondering why she was there. The woman was tall and emaciated, dressed in a loose-fitting purple nylon dress and a blue headscarf. In her hand was the panga she'd used on the farm, and her feet were covered in dust.

"You're Absalom's daughter, aren't you?" She greeted.

"Yes, that's right. Good evening. There's something I wanted to talk to you about," Akinyi said tentatively, trying to be polite.

"You're welcome to come inside." The woman led the way into the poorly lit hut. A skeletal, black dog sat by the door, yawning every few seconds.

Once seated, Akinyi went straight into the heart of the matter. "I heard about what happened to Awino."

The woman hung her head in despair, her shoulder slumped. "I will just have to marry my daughter off to that man. There is nothing I can do about it."

Akinyi was about to say something when Awino entered the room with a bucket full of water in her hand. She was a petite girl with a protruding stomach, which seemed too much for her not-so-well developed body. She extended her hand and greeted Akinyi once she put the water down, forcing a smile that didn't reach her eyes. She then took one of the stools beside her mother.

One look at the helpless duo, and Akinyi nearly screamed. Why was life so unfair?

"Awino, please tell me what happened with Ocholla?" she asked.

The young girl stared at the twisting hands on her lap, seemingly caught off-guard.

Her mother quickly stood upright, her face devoid of any trace of a smile. "Young lady, get out of my house! I know you have just come to collect gossip for your friend, Adhiambo."

Akinyi's gut congealed. "I am very sorry. That was not my reason for coming here. I want to help."

Awino's mother didn't look convinced. "Why should you even bother? Nobody cares anymore. With my husband gone, it's even worse."

The woman retook her seat. Mentioning her husband seemed to have weakened her knees.

Silence descended, Akinyi unsure of what to say.

"One day, I was going to fetch firewood," Awino broke the long silence. "When I saw Ocholla sitting outside his house. He called me, and I went to him. He then sent me into the house to bring him drinking water. Once I was inside the house, he quickly followed me and closed the door behind him. I got suspicious and asked him why he had closed the door, but he didn't answer. He moved towards me, and I moved back until my back met the wall. He grabbed me and ripped me off all my clothes. I was very scared and started shaking violently, but that did not stop him. He undid his clothes and forced himself on me."

When Awino paused, Akinyi felt warm tears cascade down her cheeks, but she didn't bother to wipe them away.

Awino continued calmly like she was sleepwalking through the whole incident. "He threatened to hurt me and my family if I told anyone or stopped going to his house for a daily dose of sex. I would go, and he would send me away with firewood so that nobody would suspect."

The girl's mother shook her head in disbelief. "That man came here last night, wanting to pay a huge sum of money for our silence. I won't lie. The money would change our lives, but at what expense?"

Akinyi did not know what to say after such a harrowing tale. The young girl sat slumped on the stool as if she had just unloaded some burden off her back. Akinyi felt like holding her and telling her it was just a bad dream and when she woke, it would be alright, but she knew that was just wishful thinking. The reality was glaring at her, and it was harsh.

Promising to do her best to help, she left them and walked home in the dark, where her mother waited impatiently by the front door.

"Since when did you become the village chief?" her mother asked, face contorted with fury.

Akinyi entered the house and settled on a squeaky stool before answering. "Since the chief stopped doing his work. All he is interested in doing is settling land disputes where he can collect kitu kidogo, little thing."

Her mother pointed a finger at her and said, "You can put that energy into use in the housework. It seems you are very idle."

Knowing the argument would get them nowhere, Akinyi ignored her and gobbled down the food. She would visit her grandmother the next day.

When she lay on the bed, sleep wouldn't come. Instead, her mind drifted to Kadogo, a seven-year-old, plump girl with the sad eyes she'd met at the Little Angel Orphanage where she volunteered.

The first day, Kadogo had clung to her hands when she'd wanted to leave, making her promise to come back. Akinyi hadn't planned on returning there soon since she'd been swamped at work and doubted whether she would find the time. She'd turned to tell the girl, but there'd been something in her eyes that day—sadness and despair.

Akinyi had nodded, and that became the start of their friendship. She'd spent her weekends at the Orphanage and discovered the girl's tragic past over time.

Kadogo had been defiled by her father, and when her mother found out, she made her swear to not tell anybody. Her keen class teacher had realized that something was off with her and went to inform her parents. In turn, her parents abandoned her in the orphanage and fled.

"I swore that I never told anyone. But they never believed me," Kadogo had whispered, tears streaming down her face.

Akinyi had hugged her. "We should report the matter to the police, you know?"

Shaking her head violently, her eyes had darted around the room. "No! If you try that, I will run away!"

"Okay, calm down. I didn't mean to scare you." Akinyi had reached for her sweaty hands. "This is your call, Kadogo."

Finally nodding, Kadogo had spoken softly. "You can't tell anyone. I just want to go home."

Akinyi kept visiting her, and they'd bonded. However, after Akinyi's father passed on, she went home and didn't visit Kadogo for a few weeks.

When she'd returned to the orphanage. The surly-faced, middle-aged man in charge had informed her that Kadogo had been found dead in her dormitory due to suicide.

She had plopped on her seat, the news knocking the wind out of her lungs, making her cold. He'd handed her a brown envelope with her name scribbled in Kadogo's handwriting. She'd eyed the letter suspiciously like it was a ticking bomb, and the coarse texture had scalded her hands. Then she'd opened it and read its contents with mounting dread, her heartbeat slowing, her breath catching. The girl had assumed she had gone for good. She'd wailed for Kadogo on the dusty orphanage floor, heartbroken.

Now, Akinyi stared at the dark, wondering why the world was so cruel to the young.

She remembered her younger years with nostalgia—carefree days full of laughter and abandon. She was fortunate.

In contrast, Kadogo and Awino wouldn't have the same. Awino would be anguished, walk around with her head bent in shame, and regard everyone, especially men, with suspicion. Would she get to fall in love and be loved after what Ocholla did?

CHAPTER SIX

Akinyi stretched on her bed the following morning, her eyes puffy and bloodshot since she got little sleep last night. Her mind had been in turmoil.

She'd thought about David, and instead of pain and desperation, hatred shook her body with its force. Who did he think he was, hurting her at the drop of a hat? She deserved better.

He'd claimed that she wasn't a 'wife material' when all she ever did was love him and take care of him when she visited him at his house within the Kahawa Army Barracks. Waiting on him for six years and all for nothing!

Tossing and turning, she berated herself for being the fool. It was men like him that turned good women into cold-hearted bitches. He could go to Hell for all she cared.

As the morning light filtered through the vents, her resolve hardened. Never again would she engage with a man in uniform. She rolled out of bed, finished her chores and left for Grandma's.

"Good morning, Nyakwara," her grandma greeted when Akinyi arrived at the shamba.

Grandma was wrinkled with white hair peeped from the scarf tied over her head. Despite being eighty-five years old, her eyes were still bright and sparkled with wisdom. She walked firmly and did her own chores. According to her, she was strong because she did not overeat Mzungu food.

"Good morning, Grandma," Akinyi answered, digging up the yams from the farm.

"How is your mother? I haven't seen her for a while," the old woman asked and continued working.

"She is fine, just upset that I want to pursue justice for Awino." Remembering the conversation with her mother, anger flared, and she threw the yam she'd dug out on the ground.

"Stop throwing the yams with much vigour!" Grandma warned, glancing at her.

"Why is that?" she retorted.

"They will become bitter when they are cooked."

"I don't believe you. Is that even possible?" It sounded ridiculous.

Her grandmother straightened. "Of course, my mother told me, and it was passed down to her by her mother."

She sighed. "Sorry, Grandma."

"It's alright. This is what you get for spending so much time in town and watching too much TV that you don't even know our beliefs," Grandma said, collecting the yams and putting them in the otheru.

Akinyi smiled as she carried the otheru and followed her to the house. They entered the well-lit mud-walled house, which smelled of soot, dry firewood, and yams. The smell was so familiar and homely, as it had always smelled since she was a little girl. The earthen floor had been swept clean, and the walls had various pictures of her grandparents in black and white.

Grandma had been a beauty in her younger years. Also, Grandpa had been quite handsome, probably why he'd won himself eight wives. In most photos, her grandmother was in short skirts and her grandfather in bell-bottom trousers and sporting thoroughly coiffed big hair.

On the wooden table, there was a jug full of porridge. Grandma poured them each a mug of the sweet and sour porridge. "Your mother doesn't want you to pursue justice for Awino, huh?"

She shook her head, and the old lady didn't speak for a long time.

"What are you thinking about, Grandma?" she asked when the silence stretched too long.

"I think your mother is right. Ocholla's sons are hell. They will harm you. Let the matter rest."

"But I want to help her since nobody wants to," Akinyi said stubbornly. Her mind flashed to Kadogo's letter. She shivered as the memory seeped cold deep into her bones.

"You know that you might eat a mango, but it's your children's teeth that decay." Grandma sipped her porridge.

"Meaning?" Akinyi asked. The old lady sometimes spoke in riddles and proverbs which eluded her.

"It means that if Ocholla is not punished for his deed right now, his children or grandchildren will pay for his mistakes."

"So, we should just wait for God to do His work?" Akinyi raised her brows.

"Exactly."

"No way, Grandma, I won't let that happen."

Grandma shook her head, humming to herself. "But our God of today is not like that of the olden days where people had to wait for ages to get punishment for their evil deeds." Looking skywards. "Our God back then used to wear robes which might have hindered his pace, but the God of today wears boxers, so the punishment comes faster than expected."

Akinyi laughed before saying, "I don't think such serious matters should be left in the hands of Fate. I will try my best to help her."

"Be careful, Nyakwara. I want to see my great-grandchildren before God calls me home."

"I will, Grandma. Let me go to the Abururu springs and fetch drinking water for you."

"Thank you, Nyakwara. God bless you."
***

Akinyi boarded a boda-boda that dropped her at the rusty Oyugis police station gate. She'd left home early in the morning after finishing her housework without informing her mother about her plans because she would object.

She knew that the locals would see her as an enemy of the people, but she didn't care. She had to act fast and save Awino lest she...She shook her head, dislodging the horror that her mind painted.

Sometimes, when pushed to the wall, with no escape, people harm themselves, just like Kadogo. It wouldn't happen again under her watch. Not if she could help it.

Strolling to the old brick building with a rusty brown roof, doubt overwhelmed. An old woman walked out, mumbling to herself, and counting her fingers. What was her story? Straightening her back, she climbed the stairs leading to the reporting office.

"Madam, how can I help you?" asked the police officer at the reception desk. He was a tall man who yawned, stretched, and seemed disinterested in his work.

Akinyi almost turned away but knew that she had to do this. Backing out was no longer an option.

"I want to report a defilement case," she said finally.

"Msichana, you are too old to be defiled," Mr Bored told her, surveying her from head to toes.

"It's not me who has been defiled but a thirteen-year-old girl in my area," you stupid moron, she wanted to add but held her tongue at the man's misogyny. She had to keep the objective in mind. Getting justice for Awino.

"And what is your relationship with this girl?" he asked.

"She is my neighbour," she answered, hating Mr Bored by the minute.

"So you are one of those nosy neighbours who put their noses where they don't belong. How does she being defiled affect you? Is the man your husband?" he asked, sneering. The officer was

40

missing some screws in his head, or his brain was upside down.

"Afande, come see this post," Mr Bored beckoned to his colleague, raising his phone. His colleague, a short man with a protruding stomach, rushed to his side, his belly wobbling. They watched whatever was on the screen, laughing, scrolling to more posts, and their laughter filled the room.

Akinyi glared at them, anger roiling inside her. The nerve of these officers. Twenty minutes later, Mr Bored looked up, scowling when he found her still rooted to the spot.

"Madam, did you say that the man is your husband?" Putting the phone in his pocket.

Akinyi's shoulders slumped as tears threatened to fill her eyes. It was just too much. She quickly walked out of the reporting room, leaving Mr Bored staring at her. Once outside, she sat on the bench, wondering what to do next. She had promised to help, and a promise was a debt.

She glanced back towards the station. One of the doors with OCS inscribed on it opened. An idea occurred to her, and she hurried towards it. She knocked, and the fat man behind the desk urged her to get in. She sat down after greeting him.

"How can I help you, madam? Have you been helped at the reporting office?" he asked.

"Not yet. I was trying to give my statement, but the officer was not interested in hearing anything I said," she explained.

Frowning, he stood from his desk and asked her to follow him to the reporting office. Mr Bored stood to attention at once and saluted his superior.

"Why have you refused to record this lady's statement?" OCS asked.

Mr Bored's eyes flew to Akinyi's accusingly. She just shrugged and smiled.

"I did not refuse, afande," he answered, almost stammering.

Akinyi almost shouted in jubilation. Who was laughing now?

"Record her statement now!" OCS ordered.

Mr Bored fumbled with his pen and recorded everything that Akinyi told him. When he was through, OCS walked with her back to his office.

"That's so brave of you. It's rare to find people who possess your courage. Most people keep such acts private, and in the end, the victim is not served justice while the perpetrator walks the streets a free man. You need to come with the defiled girl and the mother so that they can also record their statement," he said, swinging on his chair.

"I will do that. Thank you very much. I'm just trying to send a message to the perpetrators that they cannot do such things and get off the hook easily. It should also serve as a warning to others planning to do such," Akinyi said.

The OCS nodded in agreement. Akinyi stood up and left, feeling light-hearted.

CHAPTER SEVEN

Akinyi walked through the forest of about ten thousand trees as a cool breeze fanned her face. The streams of sunlight filtered through the branches.

She couldn't believe that her father had planted all these trees just ten years ago. Then people had warned him against it, claiming the trees would cause drought and dry up the neighbouring wells. Now, this forest was like a goldmine.

She felt the rough barks of the trees under her fingers, wondering why her mother was reluctant to sell the trees. The only way to get answers would be to ask her mother.

Hurrying, she arrived home and found her mother at the coop, feeding the chicken with leftover food.

"Where have you been?" her parent straightened, scowling.

What brought it on? The older woman was increasingly displeased with her.

"I went to the forest. The trees are huge. We should think of selling them." She sat on the veranda, out of breath.

"I don't want any part of that bloody money. It is the reason your father died." Nyakisumo scrubbed the water container with more vigour than required.

"What do you mean, Mama?" Akinyi asked, sitting up.

"You haven't heard that your uncle Ochal is the one who went to ajuoga to kill your father because of those trees," her mother whispered conspiratorially.

Akinyi shook her head in disbelief. "That can't be true. Baba died after being diagnosed with Diabetes. You know that."

"Akinyi, my daughter, you are still too young to understand how the world works," the woman said wistfully.

Akinyi wanted to argue but changed her mind when she saw her mother's serious expression.

Talking of the devil, Ochal passed by their fence and greeted them. "You have been so lost, my shemeji. I hope you are fine."

"We are doing great. Why don't you stop by for a mug of porridge?"

"On another day, my generous shemeji."

"You are most welcome. Give my greetings to your wife and children," Akinyi's mother said, giving him a tight smile, and he nodded, walking away.

Akinyi shook her head at the exchange and watched the retreating old man with his hunched back and walking stick. He wore his signature broad sisal hat, a pair of black trousers and a tattered white t-shirt.

Everyone in the area knew he was mean. Some people even joked that he had a snake in his pocket or that the sun never shone in his pocket. They'd nicknamed him Daktari because he claimed to have the herbs someone could use to protect the homestead from thieves.

Some praised his expertise, claiming the herbs made the thieves see a shrub instead of a house. Or that some of the herbs could even make a thief eat grass like a cow. What made him even more peculiar were the animals he possessed. All his animals were black—hens, cows, dogs, and cats.

***

"Nyakisumo, today we are going to kill your daughter! Start digging another grave." An angry voice shouted. "Why does she meddle in things that don't concern her?"

Akinyi heard a crowd shouting just outside their house early in the morning. Nyakisumo quickly got off her bed and parted the window curtains, peeping out. Akinyi tiptoed behind her and saw Ocholla's five burly sons and five boda-boda motorists outside. They were armed with pangas, machetes, and hammers. She shivered, and goosebumps formed on her arms. She wiped her sweaty palms on her nightdress.

Her mother turned back to her, looking very tired, and Akinyi could have sworn that her mother had aged right before her eyes. Her face became wrinkled, and she was slumped. Akinyi took her by the arm and led her to the bed.

"Mama, are you alright?" Akinyi asked, her heart beating frantically.

"Akinyi, my daughter, you will be the death of me," she whispered, shaking her head.

"Don't say that, Mama. I will handle this." Inner strength she didn't know she possessed surged through her, even though it warred with fear.

"How will you do that! You can hear Ocholla's sons crying for your blood." She threw her hands up in the air.

"I went looking for justice for Awino since everyone in this town wants to bury their heads in the sand. Please don't expect me to regret my actions because I don't."

"At this rate, you will end up like that chief who was butchered like a hen!" she shouted.

"It's better to die for something than live for nothing,"

Nyakisumo shook her head in protest, and tears trickled down her face.

Akinyi cursed under her breath, patting her shoulder, "Sorry, Mama, I didn't mean to make you cry."

It took a while for her mother to stop crying.

The crowd was pounding on the door and the roof, the whole house rattling under the rough treatment.

Akinyi had to act now, or things would get out of hand. She walked to the door, whispered a prayer before opening it and found Ocholla's eldest son at the forefront. His face was sweaty, and his eyes very red as if he had smoked weed before coming here. He had a sharp glittering panga in his hands.

Her blood turned ice-cold in her veins. He was very tall, towering over her, but she could not let him see her trembling out of fear. Instead, she steeled herself. She had to be strong now more than ever.

"What do you want?" she asked, hands akimbo.

The rowdy men craned their necks to see her behind the tall Ocholla's son, shouting insults at her.

"Why did you report my father to the police?" he asked, showing crooked brown teeth.

"Because that is where he needs to be for defiling a young girl," she retorted.

"Are you Awino's mother now?"

"No, but I am a member of this town."

"You should find yourself a husband to keep you busy and out of this town." His mouth twisted with distaste. "I can see you want to step on the tail of a lion. The police took my father this morning because of you,"

"Why are you blaming me for that? He is getting what he deserves. He should have kept his johnny in his boxers," Akinyi said, tapping her foot on the ground impatiently, wanting to finish this argument.

His hard slap reverberated across her right cheek, making her stagger backwards. Her mother screamed at the sound of that slap, begging Ocholla's son to have mercy on her.

"Mama, you should teach your daughter how to speak to men?" Ocholla's son roared as her mother ran out of the house.

Akinyi rubbed her hot, stinging cheek and spat on Ocholla's son's face.

His face contorted in anger before he yanked her off her feet like she was paperweight and threw her into the waiting mob. She tried to fight him off, punching his back and kicking in the air, but he didn't let go. If at all, he only tightened his vicelike grip on her, bruising her, pain radiating through her.

CHAPTER EIGHT

Adams was driving by Akinyi's home to Kisumu when he heard the ear-piercing wail coming from the compound. Stopping the car abruptly, he rushed into the premises, his stomach churning with dread.

"You fools, stop!" Adams bellowed.

The mob turned to look at him, panting like rabid dogs. One of the men halted his panga in mid-air above Akinyi's head. Her mother was atop her, trying to protect her daughter.

The men didn't seem to care. It looked like they would lynch mother and daughter. What the hell?

"Who is this?" They murmured among themselves, looking like they would attack him too.

He didn't care. What had the world become when grown men would beat on women? He'd joined the military to protect the innocent, and he certainly wouldn't let these buffoons hurt these two.

"What the hell do you think you are doing, beating two helpless women?" He moved towards the crowd, body alert, staying watchful for sudden movements.

"And who do you think you are, sticking your nose where it doesn't belong?" Ocholla's eldest son stepped forward, sticking his chest out. He raised his panga.

Big mistake.

Instinctively, Adams hit the man's wrist hard, sending the weapon flying in the air. Giving in to the violent storm raging inside him, he lowered his body and swiped the man off his feet, making the idiot land his butt on the ground and groan in pain. Then, two more fell from his roundhouse kicks, and he slapped a fourth into a stupor. The others ran away after witnessing what had happened to their friends. The ones who had been knocked to the ground scrambled and crawled to get away.

Silence ensued as the older woman watched in helpless fascination while the last of the mob departed through the gate.

Akinyi lay in a pool of blood, unconscious, with clothes soaked in blood.

Adams dropped to his knees beside her, heart racing, adrenaline still high. "We need to get her to the hospital."

He checked her pulse rate and found it weak, and she was losing blood. He lifted her, carrying her to his car while her mother followed closely behind him, limping.

He drove quickly to Matata hospital and handed her to the casualty section. The nurses rushed forth and put her on a stretcher, wheeling her into the ward. Adams sat on the edge of his seat, rubbing his hands together. Nyakisumo couldn't keep still. She kept pacing to the door they had wheeled Akinyi into as if to listen through the entrance.

After what seemed like an eternity, a short doctor with a smiley face and hair sprinkled with grey approached them. They quickly stood up, closing the distance.

"Doctor, how is she?" Nyakisumo blurted.

"Good evening, Mama. Akinyi is stable now and is responding to the medication we have administered so far."

Nyakisumo heaved a sigh of relief, mirroring Adam's feeling. His stomach had been in knots, and the tension eased with the good news.

"Thank God! Can we see her?" she rushed to ask.

"Of course. But wait until they finish running tests on her." He adjusted the dangling stethoscope on his neck. "The nurse-in-charge will update you on the progress."

Bidding them farewell, his shoes echoed in the empty corridor.

Nyakisumo resumed her pacing, wearing the floor out as she mumbled incoherently under her breath.

Adams tried to get her to sit down, but she declined. She had had minor bruises on her arms which had been attended to by the nurses. He went to the hospital canteen and bought milk, so she would sit for a while to drink it.

"I am not hungry. The only thing that matters now is for my daughter to be well," she said softly.

When he listened keenly to her mumblings, he realized they were prayers. So he didn't disturb her again until lunchtime. This time she agreed to eat something. Afterwards, he left, promising to return later.

He went back to the hospital in the evening.

Akinyi was in the ward, wrapped in bandages on the head, face and arms, sleeping peacefully. She had been injected with a sedative. Her mother was on the chair next to the bed, dozing, her neck hanging awkwardly off the seat. He tapped her lightly on the shoulder. She woke with a start, groaning and rubbing the back of her neck.

"Please go home. I will stay with her for the night," Adams said.

She shook her head violently. "I have to be here. After all that you have done for us, I can't burden you. What is your name?"

"Adams Okal, ma'am. I'm Akinyi's friend."

"Thank you again for your help and courage today. May God reward you!" She extended her hand in greeting.

"It was nothing. You need some rest. Please go home," Adams pleaded, reaching for her outstretched hand.

"He is right, Mama. Go home." Akinyi opened her swollen eyes, making them turn in her direction.

Adams swallowed the lump in his throat, eyeing her with concern.

"Akinyi!" Nyakisumo stood up and embraced her, careful not to squeeze her. She lifted her head, and they both had tears in their eyes. She resettled in her chair, tracing fingers on her daughter's bandages, voice cracking. "How are you feeling?"

"I am feeling alright. Mama." Akinyi dabbed her tears with her bedsheet. "A little pain here and there, but I will be okay."

"Oh, my daughter. Ocholla's sons wanted to send my only source of joy to the afterlife." Tears flowed down her mother's face.

"Mama, please don't cry. I am fine." Akinyi outstretched her bandaged hand and patted her mother's arm.

Her mother nodded after a while, sucking in a deep breath, and Akinyi laughed shakily.

"Will you be alright if I leave you with him for the night?" The older woman adjusted the bed cover.

"Of course, Mama, you should go home," Akinyi said, injecting enthusiasm into her voice.

Her mother cast weary glances between her daughter and Adams. Then eventually, she promised to return before the cock crows and left. As the door closed behind her, Adams moved from the middle of the room and sat in the chair her mother had vacated.

"How are you feeling for real?" he asked, his voice a whisper.

"Not so good. I feel pain all over my body, and the painkillers aren't helping," she confessed, looking so small and helpless that it tugged at Adams' heart.

He took her swollen right hand into his, caressing it gently as he stared at her tenderly.

Her gaze skittered around the room, not meeting his. Was she shy?

He lifted her hand to his lips and kissed the knuckles through the bandage as he looked deep into her eyes. Her eyes widened as her gaze finally landed on him. He chuckled under his breath, keeping her hands in his.

"Don't you have someone waiting for you at home?" she blurted, pulling her hands away. "I don't want to cause drama."

"No one," he said tersely, clenching his jaws, wondering where this conversation was headed.

"Maybe a wife and half a dozen children?" she asked, raising her left eyebrow.

"No," he answered, smiling.

"Ooh, then. Are you widowed?"

"No."

"Are you divorced?" She was unrelenting.

"No, Akinyi," he said, her name rolling out of his tongue like a caress.

"Ok, I give up," she said, shifting on the bed to lie on her side.

"You want to know something simple, yet you are going round and round,"

"You know if I ask plainly if you are married, you will think I want to ensnare you."

She hid her face with her sheet as Adams' laughter echoed in the room. The potent throaty sound settled on her stomach, releasing a swarm of butterflies swirling inside her. That sound was deadly to a woman trying to protect her heart.

"Let me save you further inquiries. I am very single and ready to mingle," he said.

"All men are always single," she countered, rolling her eyes.

"I am. Trust me," he said earnestly, holding her gaze.

"I find that hard to believe," she said, her lingering stare roaming over his body.

He shifted on his seat as her heated gaze wrapped him up, warming him, causing his dick to stir to life.

"Why?" he asked, chuckling under his breath, acting nonchalant when all he wanted to do was tell her to keep devouring him in her eyes. He wanted to bask in the glory of her hot gaze.

"With a body and a face like yours, you must have a crowd of women camping outside your door, and you have to shoo them away with a stick." She stared at her toes, blushing like hell.

He was convinced that the attraction was mutual.

"Stop exaggerating. I am just a normal guy," he said, shaking his head in disbelief. He realized she was fatigued by how she stifled a yawn that tears came to her eyes. She needed to rest.

"Sleep now. We will continue with our banter tomorrow." He leaned over and covered her with the bedding.

Her eyes drifted shut, and her breathing pattern became regular.

Watching her, the pang in his chest returned. He wished he lay in the bed in her stead, injured. He wanted to protect this woman not only from the Ocholla boys but forever from all the world's dangers. The notion troubled him. He didn't know her that well, yet he felt compelled to do so, like it was why he was put on earth, like a dedication to the oath he took in the army.

He walked out of the hospital, the evening air cool, the crickets' singsong soothing. Plopping onto a deserted bench, he breathed in and out to clear his mind. And when he was finally able to relax, he looked up to the starry night, partaking in the simple pleasure of nature. It then came to him that he would rather be here in the hospital with her than be anywhere else.

CHAPTER NINE

Akinyi woke the next day feeling groggy. Her whole body ached, and she groaned in pain when she tried to stretch on the bed. She tried to open her eyes but squinted due to the harsh bright light.

Adams sat in the chair, sleeping. She hadn't heard him come back, but she was glad that he was here. She tapped his leg, and he stirred awake, his eyes red.

"Good morning," Akinyi greeted, and he murmured something incoherent.

The doctor came, checked her vitals and announced that she could go home in the afternoon. Akinyi almost jumped from bed with joy. and her happiness was infectious.

Adams' face lit up with a smile. "What do you want for breakfast, Jaber?"

"Milk," she replied.

"I will be back in a minute," he announced, leaving the room.

Akinyi drank water from a cup on the bedside table. She was just standing up to go to the toilet when someone came in.

"Nyakwara, I am so sorry," Grandma said, hugging her.

She felt warm in the embrace, basking in the familiar scent of wood smoke and the earth of her granny.

When they parted, she proceeded to the toilet. Every part of her body was aching, especially around the stitches. When she came limping back into the ward, she found Grandma and Adams talking in hushed tones.

They stopped talking when they saw her. Her grandma helped her to her bed. After she was tucked in bed, Grandma said, "Adams was just telling me that he found the Ocholla boys assaulting you."

The image flashed before her, making her dizzy and nauseous. She closed her eyes, wishing them away. She couldn't shake the horror she'd felt, the helplessness, the despair, the immeasurable pain that rattled her bones.

"That's over now, Grandma. Adams saved us in time." She smiled weakly, opening her eyes.

"What if he hadn't arrived in time?" Grandma asked, shaking her head. "I went for fellowship, and I was told of the news on coming back. Yesternight I had a weird dream and didn't know what to make of it."

"Sorry, Grandma. I didn't mean to trouble you."

"It's alright, Nyakwara. That was brave of you." She tapped lightly on her leg.

The doctor came back and announced that she could be discharged.

Akinyi smiled, swinging her legs to the floor and asked her Grandma to help her change into her clothes.

"Let me go and process your discharge," Adams announced, leaving the room.

"Thank you very much, Okal," Grandma said.

Adams nodded, going out the door.

"I like this young man," Grandma said, her eyes lighting up with mischief. "I think he's in love with you."

"Come on, Grandma! I barely know him." Akinyi put on her slippers.

Grandma snickered, taking her leso from the rail. "Continue telling yourself that lie. I have seen how you look at him."

"How do I look at him?" Akinyi ventured, dreading that her all-knowing Grandma had seen through her veil of attraction to Adams. But who would blame her when the man was a walking testosterone bomb, commanding the gazes of everyone to give him a second glance.

"Like you want to eat him for lunch." Grandma's eyes danced with naughtiness. Akinyi broke into a loud laugh as her grandma chuckled. "You know I am right."

Akinyi didn't give in nor deny it. Instead, she mulled over her grandmother's words. Adams was a puzzle waiting to be explored.

Grandma quickly helped her change and shoved her items into a bag.

Adams breezed into the room with the discharge form as they were finishing up.

"That was fast. I forgot to give you my National Identity card. Here," Akinyi handed him the card.

"No need for that. I have sorted it out." He took her bags.

"What! You didn't have to." Akinyi gasped, mortified.

"I know. I wanted to." He walked out of the room, leaving them open-mouthed, staring at his back as if it held the answers.

Grandma's gaze shifted to her face, reading her. She shrugged, sure that her face mirrored what was deeply entrenched in her heart. Adams was making it difficult not to fall for him, fast and hard.

Adams drove them home in his car, dust billowing in their wake. He parked the car outside her house and helped Akinyi into the house and onto the sofa.

"Thank you, young man," Grandma said, shaking Adams' hand firmly that Akinyi had to smile. Grandma had more strength confined in her petite frame.

Akinyi mouthed 'thank you' to him.

He nodded, turning down their offer to stay for tea.

***

"Good morning Nyakwara. I brought you the herbs," Grandma said, pouring the green potion into a white cup.

She woke up with a start, the scent of fresh herbs hugging the room. Her grandma had insisted on boiling bitter herbs for her faster recovery. It had been like this for days. Every morning Grandma showed up with the herbal drinks.

Akinyi winced, suppressing the urge to crawl under the blanket and disappear. She tightly closed her eyes and faked a snore.

"Stop being smart with me. Wake up," Grandma said, nudging her. "I have treated a lot of people with this potion."

She held out the cup in Akinyi's face. The smell hit her nose, and she sneezed three times, the force shaking her body. She winced in pain

"I told you. Your grandma, the town healer, makes potent stuff." She nodded, pride in her eyes.

Akinyi quickly gulped the medicine, her eyes closed. It burnt its way down to her stomach, the bitter taste lasting long after she placed the cup on the table. Her stomach growled as she reached for water to chase the tart taste.

Grandma rubbed her back.

"I will now tend to your wounds," she said, gently removing her clothes to bare the healing cuts. Her grandma wiped the wounds with a towel which she dipped in the green water. When she finished, Akinyi thanked her, pulling on the dress.

"It's nothing. I am here for you. I will come back in the evening." The old woman smiled, stowing away the remains of the herbs.

She rolled her eyes, and Grandma laughed, shuffling out of the room.

Tired of lying down, she wanted to be on her feet already. Her right cheek still bore a big scar from the panga. Grandma kept promising that if she drank the herbs, she would be as smooth as a baby's butt in a month. She slept for a while, dreading the evening when the woman would return with more bitter herbs.

"Awino and her mother are here to see you," her mother announced, placing fermented porridge on the stool.

Akinyi sat up on the bed as the young girl and her mother walked in hesitantly.

Awino stood in the middle of the room while her mother sat in the plastic chair by her bed.

"Awino, take this seat." Akinyi pointed at the empty one next to her mother's.

Chewing on her lips, the girl sat with her body facing the door as if ready to bolt.

"How are you feeling?" Awino's mother asked, extending her hand in greeting.

"I am healing," Akinyi said, rubbing her eyes.

"We heard what the Ocholla sons did to you. I am so sorry."

Akinyi shrugged, "The worst has passed. You were brave to back up my statement at the police station."

"But I feel awful. Look at you, all bruised because of us." Concerned eyes pierced hers.

"It's fine. Ocholla is behind bars, and his sons and the rogue boda-boda riders have been rounded up, facing charges of assault. They will not dare come near you or me."

"Thank you. Without you, I don't know what we would have done," Awino's mother said, holding Awino's hand tenderly.

"You are welcome. How are you, Awino?"

"I am fine. Thank you," Awino replied, looking at her through hollow eyes, and shifting on her seat.

Akinyi wished again that she could take all Awino's pain away. The girl was too young to be exposed to the world's craziness. Her stomach also protruded from the T-shirt, with many holes baring her skin.

"We don't want to keep you awake. Rest now," Awino's mother said, getting up.

Awino gave her a ghost of a smile as she walked out of the room.

For the first time, Akinyi knew that all was not lost. But still, a lot had to be done. From the look of her stomach, Awino was about seven months pregnant. Akinyi just hoped that she would be able to continue with her schooling after the baby arrived.

CHAPTER TEN

After two weeks, Akinyi woke up, her body healing well. Although the scars were slightly visible, she was strong enough to work around the house.

Wondering why Adams hadn't shown up again, she decided to go and look for him.

She boarded a boda-boda which took her to his doorstep. She got off the motorbike, slightly dizzy. She wasn't as strong as she thought. The compound was in a flurry of activities. The mansion was at the roof level. The only thing remaining was the roofing and the finishing. She could tell that the house was big, about eight rooms. She was still looking at the home when he emerged from the group of workers.

Akinyi's heart stopped beating as she watched him approach in a dazed stupor. She drank in his appearance as he strutted to her, holding her gaze. His powerful stride reminded her of an African warrior. He was bare-chested, his broad chest tapering to a thin waist. He didn't even have a trace of fat in that flat stomach, and his faded pair of jeans rode low on his waist, revealing the top of his white pair of boxers. What kind of a man wears white boxers?

"Good afternoon, Jaber. What a pleasant surprise!" he said, extending his hand.

She could not summon an answer immediately, her brain refusing to form words.

"Good afternoon," she said distractedly when he looked at her with a raised eyebrow, awaiting her response. His skin was glistening with sweat, his tight nipples begging to be sucked. Goodness! What was wrong with her? She suddenly had the urge to scratch her neck.

She stood there stupefied, looking at the ground, almost drawing the Kenyan map with her toes, his musky scent wrapping her in a halo of lust.

"Akinyi, are you okay?" he called out her name, touching her hand.

Dragging her gaze from the ground, she met his concerned eyes.

She nodded, not trusting her vocal codes.

Quickly grabbing his shirt from his shoulder, he wore it mumbling something like, "where are my manners." Not that she was listening.

Her brain had taken a vacation, leaving her with an empty skull. She had seen naked men before. What was wrong with her? But this man was simply different, so perfect. She crossed her hands behind her back lest she reached out and ran them over his chest, tracing the abs.

"I can see you are healing well," Adams said, leading her to the shade under the tree. They sat down on the wooden seats under the shade. The breeze fanned her face, and she felt the feverish heat that had crept through her body start to cool.

"I came to thank you for saving us."

"The pleasure was all mine."

"My mother told me that you gave the mob quite a beating that they crawled out the gate." She couldn't contain the giggle escaping her lips.

The horror had dissipated, and she was at a place where she could make fun of the ordeal.

His mouth twitched into a smile, "They needed someone to drive sense into their thick heads."

Silence fell as they eyed each other, no one in the mood to break it. Why again was she here?

"I won't keep you from your work. I am going home," she announced, getting up. Though, she wanted to stay and talk all day long, watch that smile, ogle that body, run her hands all over his skin …

"You are not keeping me from anything. Let me rustle up some juice," he said, pulling at her hand lightly so that she could sit down.

The touch lingered long after, a promising contact. She sat down as he went into the small brick makeshift house a few meters from the mansion.

He came back with a jug full of freshly blended mango juice. Once they had a glass each, she caught him looking at her and looked away, feeling self-conscious. She had been around the block long enough to know what the look was conveying. The air crackled with the chemistry between them.

"So, what have you been up to all week?" she asked, just to fill the lull in the conversation.

"Not much. I have been busy with the house. I want to finish it by next month." He motioned to the building.

"How many rooms does it have?"

"Eight rooms."

"That's too big for one person." She noted idly.

"It is. I love lots of space."

"Your family will be visiting?" she asked, sipping her juice and liking how it cooled her inside out.

Adams stiffened, taking a long gulp of his drink. "Maybe."

She was tempted to pursue that line of conversation, but when she saw him sit up stiffly, clenching and unclenching his jaw, she let it rest.

What had happened to his family? Was there a problem? Was that why he was building his ranch miles from home? Was he running away from something or someone?

It was none of her business, but she couldn't help wondering. This man had saved her life, and it was only logical to be concerned about him. Plus, this thing between them was just ... She raised her hand and touched her healing face, a reminder that she should always mind her own business.

They talked some more before she announced that she had to leave. It was almost getting dark, the sun sinking below God Wire.

"I will drive you home," he announced, taking their empty glasses into the house.

She stared after him, still wondering. It seemed her question had annoyed him, breaking his mellow mood.

He came back with the car keys, and they left. She realized that he was preoccupied with his thoughts, and she didn't blabber until they reached her home.

The neighbours strained their eyes to better look at the car occupants. This would give them juicy gossip. People had nothing else to do than talk about their folks in a small town. In fact, they didn't call it gossip. They called it 'checking up on the neighbours.'

She thanked him and walked into her home. Feeling his eyes appraising her, she glanced at him over her shoulder and waved. He waved back, looking forlorn and so out of place. She was tempted to run back to him and hug him or, better yet, kiss him.

What was his story? She wondered as she joined her mother in the kitchen.

***

Adams waited until Akinyi disappeared into the compound before starting the drive home. He was sorry for being moody after she asked about his family, but it was still a raw subject. He wanted to escape from it all and pretend it didn't exist.

He drove at a slow speed taking in his surroundings. The children walking home from school, the women rushing home with baskets of groceries or buckets full of water. The men sitting at Agawo si Kenya discussing 'serious matters' like Raila Agwambo's chances of becoming the president while sipping sodas before going home later.

It was such an ordinary evening, but it made him smile. While in Somalia, such events had been rare. He had often wished for normalcy, but he had been disappointed there. Now, a typical evening seemed like a present wrapped with a ribbon, and he didn't take it for granted.

Still, he couldn't shake the loneliness, boredom, emptiness, and restlessness taking a permanent residence in his heart, body, and soul.

Everyone needed a partner, a companion.

He envied the men walking home with the promise of a hot meal and warm body. A potential of smooth, soft thighs, of tunnelling into sweet, wet pussy. To lose themselves and forget the worries of this life for a few blissful moments.

Oh, God, he needed that with a hunger that went bone-deep. He needed a woman in his life. His throbbing dick reminded him of its existence, unmet needs, and neglect. He wondered what it would be like to touch Akinyi, to kiss her lips and body. He wiped his sweaty face, his body heating up just from the mere thought. What would it feel like to crawl into her body, connect with her soul, and brand her as his?

***

Akinyi was washing utensils outside her house when Adhiambo showed up.

"Good morning," her friend said, getting closer. "I heard what happened. I am so sorry."

"Thank you. Where have you been?" Akinyi carried the utensils back into the house.

"I was called abruptly to go and take care of my sick sister, Atieno, in Kanyamwa."

"Sorry. How is she now?"

"She died." Tears filled Adhiambo's eyes.

"That's sad. I'm sorry."

"She left three children; two girls and a boy."

"Who is going to take care of them?"

"I was told that I have to marry the man and help him take care of the children."

"And you refused, right?"

Her friend just shrugged. "What choice do I have? Remain in this town and die an old spinster as the people ridicule me?"

"Adhiambo, don't do this! You will get a man, don't rush into this," Akinyi said, holding her hand.

"No, I am tired of waiting for Mr Right. My sister always said that the man treated her right. I hope he will do the same for me."

"Then your mind is made up?"

Adhiambo nodded, smiling. "I heard that you have been getting cosy with the Prado man."

Akinyi laughed. "I thought you came back to this village today."

"Yes, but you know that I have to get updated on what I missed. I saw how the man was looking at you that day...."

"How was he looking at me?"

"Don't pretend you didn't notice. I think you will make a lovely couple."

"Who said we were getting married?"

"Me. Go for it. You aren't getting any younger."

"Maybe I will. When are you leaving?"

"Next week. There is a disco matanga at Bongu. Please promise me that we will go."

Akinyi shook her head in disbelief. "I am not feeling well."

"You are lying. Your wounds are over-healed." Adhiambo laughed.

Akinyi still could not understand why the locals saw funerals as a celebration. Apart from gossip, funerals were right at the top of recreational activities. She'd gone to the disco matangas as a young girl, but she felt too old now.

"Please, let's have fun before I leave."

Fun? She couldn't help but wonder at Adhiambo's definition of fun. Of course, having fun at someone's funeral was gross. But again, her friend was leaving, and things wouldn't be the same.

She had seen relationships nosedive when her college friends got married. It was like they were communicating on different frequencies, living on other planets. While Akinyi talked about hot men and partying, they usually talked about babies, husbands, clinics, and in-laws. After a while, it became apparent that they were in different worlds. The distance had gotten so huge that it became a gaping hole. She had then decided to hang out with her single friends.

"I will try my best."

"Let's leave at 9 o'clock," Adhiambo sounded excited as she departed.

Akinyi watched her leave and felt at a loss, sadness and loneliness creeping over her. She would miss her friend.

"Are you alright?" Her mother approached with a basket full of groceries, which she dropped on the kitchen table.

"Yes, mother. Just sad that Adhiambo is leaving," she mentioned Adhiambo's plans to marry the widowed brother-in-law.

"You should be happy for her," her mother urged.

"I am happy for her. It's just that I will miss her very much."

"But she will visit once in a while."

"I don't want things to change. I just want her to be here."

Her mother chuckled before saying, "Nothing remains the same, my daughter. Change is the only constant thing in this world. You will get over it, trust me."

Akinyi looked at her, confused. Get over it? Was her mother speaking about her or herself?

"Take this omena and start preparing it. I'm going to take a bath," her mother announced, entering the house.

Akinyi quickly prepared supper. When she finished, she got ready for the disco matanga. However, she wasn't that enthusiastic about it. After supper, Adhiambo arrived with two of her older brothers armed with pangas. Seeing that they were in safe hands, her mother told them to have fun.

CHAPTER ELEVEN

Akinyi and Adhiambo walked the distance to Bongu, chatting. The night air was cool, the half-moon high in the sky. The air smelled of Moringa blossoms.

The sound of gospel music reached them before they entered the venue. People stood in small groups, chattering. A preacher strained to be heard above the ruckus, droning on about Heaven and Hell. The locals were obviously not interested in listening to "...the good going to Heaven while the sinners go to Hell." It was a losing battle.

The adolescents hid in the dark, drinking shakers and chwakramyacin. Some could also be heard giggling in the grassy field, making out. The drunkards were shouting that they wanted the secular songs of Johnny Junior, Atomi Sifa and Emma Jalamo. When it got to midnight, their pleas were granted. They entered the dance floor, the boys holding the girls on the waist. Finally, the adults left for bed. This was now a youth event.

Akinyi found a chair and sat in the tent, watching, amused.

"Let's go dance," Adhiambo urged her.

She shook her head and watched her friend on the dance floor with one of the town boys she used to date. Akinyi didn't know why she was reluctant to join. After going to college, this wasn't an event that appealed to her. She didn't feel part of the celebration.

Instead, she swatted the numerous mosquitoes feasting on her. This had been a bad idea. She should have stayed at home. Unfortunately, it was too late to go home by herself now.

Adhiambo came back sweating and happy. "That was quite a dance. That man can make a woman sweat."

"Are you talking about the dance?" Akinyi asked, frowning.

"Of course. What else would I be talking about?" Adhiambo replied, breaking into a loud laugh. "He was my first love. When you farm, you start with nyakrundu, the kitchen garden."

Akinyi couldn't contain her smile. "That was your nyakrundu."

"Yeah, too bad we can't marry each other because we are both from Rachuonyo."

"Yes, my dear. Have fun with him for the last time. After today, no more disco matanga, no Nyakrundu."

"I know. Tonight is the last night for all good things to end," Adhiambo said wistfully. Still, when Johnny Junior's Adongo song came on, she searched for her nyakrundu on the dance floor.

Akinyi remained in the tent, listening to the music and nodding.

"It seems that someone is bored," Adams announced, sitting next to her, his baritone rumbling through her body.

Akinyi looked up at him, grinning. "What are you doing here? You don't strike me as the kind to attend such events."

"The man was one of us."

"One of you?" she asked, confused.

"He was a soldier based in Somalia."

"What!"

"Yes. He even told me where I could get suitable land for my ranch."

Akinyi was still reeling from the waterfall of information. Adams was a soldier. The reality of the words sank deeply. She had her eyes set on a soldier again! How foolish could she get? Soldiers were heartbreakers and were to be avoided.

"What's wrong?"

"Nothing, I just feel sleepy."

"I can take you home if you want."

"Let me inform my friend," she said, standing up.

She scanned the dance floor but saw no sign of Adhiambo. Instead, she found her friend behind the house engaged in a lip-locking battle that was sure to lead to the grass. They were tearing at each other's clothes and taking everything as if there was no tomorrow. And there truly wasn't. She wasn't in the mood to interrupt the occasion. She wasn't also into voyeurism, so she left. She met one of her friend's brothers and informed him of her departure.

"Let's go," she informed Adams.

Why did he have to be another man in uniform? The thought plagued her as they travelled towards her house.

***

When Adams received news of the fallen soldiers, he had felt a knife turn in his heart. He had come to see the fellow soldiers as more than friends, more like brothers. They always looked out for each other, watching each other's backs.

What had been more disheartening was that most of those who had died had been in his platoon. And if he hadn't quit, maybe he would have been dead too. The thought alone sent chills down his spine. The fallen soldiers didn't deserve this. He lit a cigarette and watched the smoke rise into the air. The smoke felt like life, here today and gone the next minute like it never existed.

He remembered how Oti used to talk about his wife. He'd always been glad to go home and would return to the frontline with a glow in his eyes that lasted for many days. Adams had secretly envied him, envied his source of comfort and happiness away from all the war.

He remembered one story Oti had narrated that had stuck with him all these years. It had been one of the nights that they'd made a bonfire and drunk beer while feasting on roasted meat. Oti had gone home for leave after five months of not seeing his wife. He'd arrived home and found the wife outside relaxing. He'd carried her into the house and made love to her as if his life depended on it, his bag still on his back, boots and clothes on.

They had laughed at the tale. Adams had longed for someone like that, willing to wait and put up with all the stresses of army life.

The loneliness crept back. He'd managed to keep it under leash, but tonight it just had its own will. He could have died without a wife or a child. Then he would be forgotten like some writing on the sand, washed away by the ocean. He was on his dream ranch all alone. So much for wanting some peace of mind.

In the army, they always had each other. Out here, he was on his own. The silence was deafening. He quickly downed his bottle of Tusker and felt good as it burned its way to his stomach. He hated his life, hated being alone and lonely.

Everyone needed someone, he mused, rocking on his chair. Unfortunately, the cool Kachieng' night did nothing to assuage his pain.

***

"Good morning," Adhiambo greeted as she grabbed her jerrican at the spring the following day.

"Good morning, Mrs Nyakrundu," Akinyi replied, smiling.

"Stop teasing me about that."

"I was just saying. It seems you had yourself a wonderful night."

"I did. It was so refreshing. Now I am ready to get married and be faithful."

Akinyi couldn't help laughing. "Yesterday, I didn't get to ask, the man who died was he in the army?"

"Yes. He was based in Somalia. I heard that their camp was attacked by the Al-Shabaab militants, and everyone was wiped out."

"So sad, but the news reported that only a few were killed."

Adhiambo shrugged. "His wife has been crying for days on end."

"I guess it's only a widow who knows the pain of losing a husband."

"The body is being brought tomorrow and will be buried on Saturday. I hope we will attend the funeral. The whole town will be there. I have heard that there will be a lorry full of the army men, and they will be firing guns."

"It sounds like it will be fun then," Akinyi said, winking at her.

"That means that you will be attending?"

"I guess so." They filled their jerricans and set for home.

CHAPTER TWELVE

On the burial day, Oti's home was a flurry of activities. The tents were packed. The men in uniform were all over the compound. Adhiambo kept nudging Akinyi when she saw the tall, handsome ones looking their way.

"They are so handsome. I am spoilt for choice," Adhiambo whispered excitedly.

"You can take the lorry full of them and hide them under your bed," Akinyi teased with a wink.

"There goes the one I told you had a dimple." Her friend smiled invitingly at the man.

Akinyi had to suppress the laughter bubbling in her.

Different people gave testimonies of how they had adored Oti. Adams mingled easily with the army men, chatting, laughing, and shaking hands. He hadn't been lying. He was indeed one of them. It now made sense, the way he had handled Ocholla's sons.

Oti's colleagues were given a chance to eulogise. Adams walked to the podium when it was his turn.

"Oti, as we called him in the army, was a close friend of mine. He was the one who led me here when I told him that I needed a quiet place to retire. I am deeply sorry for his family...." He looked like he wanted to add more but changed his mind and walked back to his seat.

Silence descended as the widow walked to the podium. The wife's testimony was always the highlight of local funerals. It gave the people something to talk about. This one spoke about their endless love and regret for losing the love of her life.

The local politicians wooed the people to vote for them in the next elections, pledging to build roads and schools, and support the orphans. And like the previous pledges, the natives knew the words would remain unfulfilled. During the harambee, money was collected that filled the basin until a second basin had to be brought. Some people watched the large collection bowls enviously and murmured, "I wish I could be given a handful of that."

When it was time to bury, the soldiers marched alongside the pallbearers to the grave. They then fired the twenty-one-gun salute for the fallen hero. The locals stood in awe, some old women screaming, little children wailing, others watching the spectacle.

People departed when it was all over, and others went to queue for food. Some people complained that they had been given little ugali or chicken wings. Some went to queue for second servings. Some grouched about leaving on empty stomachs, yet they could still see some cows in the compound.

Adams bade the soldiers goodbye and went home. He needed to be alone, to mourn his friend in private. When he got home, darkness had descended on earth like a blanket. The crickets were chirping. He brought the beer and cigarette outside and sat on the rocking chair. He lit the cigarette and watched it burn before starting to smoke it. The warmth it brought chased the night chill away. He was about to light the second cigarette when he realized that he wasn't alone.

"Who is there?" Squinting into the dark, his body coiled to attention, prepping for an attack.

"It's me." Akinyi sashayed into the light, and he was tempted to believe that he had never seen such a beautiful woman.

"Hi," she whispered, closing the distance.

"Hi, what are you doing here so late, Akinyi?" he asked, tapping the space on the seat next to him.

"I am asking myself the same question, especially after I swore never to associate with men in uniform." She sat down, her rosy perfume enveloping him.

"Is that so?" he said, chuckling.

"Yes. I thought you needed someone to talk to."

"You thought right. Can I bring you a soda?" he asked, getting up.

"That would be lovely."

"I didn't know that you smoke." She pointed at the packet of cigarettes and lighter on the stool.

"Sorry for that. It is some stupid habit I picked up in the army," he said, putting out the cigarette he still had between his fingers.

She sipped her soda, looking out into the sky. The night was moonless, with only the stars lighting the sky. They sat for a while, not talking. Instead of thinking about the unfairness of life, Adams was drawn to the beauty beside him.

"So, you are a retired soldier?" she asked, but it was more of a statement than a question.

"I am. Does that surprise you?"

She nodded. "I can't picture you in a uniform and carrying a gun."

He shrugged before saying, "Looks can be deceiving."

They sat in the silence, watching the night pass, neither of them in a rush to fill in the silence. Just knowing that the other person was around was enough, so comforting.

Adams didn't know how to repay her for showing up tonight.

The full moon appeared from behind a cloud, illuminating the earth. The air was fresher and scented with Moringa. A moth played around the light bulb, and crickets chirped ceaselessly.

Akinyi swatted the mosquitoes that had become vicious in their biting, shifting on her seat.

"I should probably get going," she announced, emptying her glass.

He looked up at her and wondered what it would feel like if she spent the night. He wondered what it would feel like to make love to her, hold her and kiss her. He shook his head, smiling. It was the beer or the loneliness making him have such thoughts.

A look at his watch revealed that it was fifteen minutes past nine. He led the way to his car and drove her home. The sweet flowery scent of her perfume filled the car, making him so aware of her. Her shadowy figure beside him looked so sensual that he was tempted to reach out and touch her. Still, his hands remained firmly on the steering wheel, his knuckles white from the restraint.

When they got to the gate, he stopped the car. She was about to jump out and rush to bed when he reached for her hand.

"Thank you for coming," he whispered.

She felt his thumb caressing her hand. For a moment, her throat couldn't coordinate with her brain to respond. This wasn't good, getting warm with a man in his car. She gently withdrew her hand from his.

"You are welcome," she said, opening her door.

He wished her goodnight and drove home.

***

Adams invited the neighbours for his housewarming party. They arrived in droves since it was the month of May, and most folks had drained their granaries of the January harvest. It was a relief that someone could provide for even one meal. Some people ate way too much and even took some home.

Most girls paraded around the compound, trying to get his attention. Who didn't want to be swept away by a wealthy prince charming? Adams couldn't stop smiling at their advances.

"Interesting, huh?" Akinyi said, now standing by his side.

"It seems I am a hot cake. Every girl is trying to impress me."

"Lucky you. You should jump at the opportunity."

"I like to hunt."

"Is that so?"

"Yes. This is like dropping a dead mongoose on my doorstep," he said, motioning at the girls.

She smiled, shaking her head. "Mr Hunter, they are here. You can chase them and see who runs the fastest."

"No. Something tells me that they would let me catch them even if I tried to chase them. That doesn't intrigue me much. I want someone who can give me a good run," he said, eyeing her.

One of the elders approached them, and she took that as a cue to escape. At around 6 o'clock, the visitors started to disperse. The dark clouds and the thunder's rumbling made the women leave earlier, announcing that they had to go unhang clothes from the cloth line or remove maize left to dry in the sun.

***

When it got to 7 o'clock, everyone had left except Akinyi. She told herself that the drizzle had just started, and she didn't want to be rained on. Yet, deep inside, she knew she had remained to spend time alone with Adams. She hadn't expected to like him this much. But with every passing moment, every heartbeat, he kept pulling her heartstrings.

It started raining like the gods were angry, hailstones beating the roof ferociously.

Akinyi paced the room where she'd taken shelter, staring out the window for the umpteenth time. It had been raining for the past half an hour and still nowhere near stopping. It was now dark, and lightning illuminated the candlelit house every now and then. This was followed by loud claps of thunder that made her shiver with dread. She hated thunderstorms.

She crossed her arms over her chest as she stood by the window. Adams had gone to prepare the tea. Her heart skipped when she heard his footsteps approaching, but she didn't turn to look at him. Her body hummed with need, and she felt like Icarus. Was she flying too close to the sun in her waxed wings?

He got closer, wrapping his muscular arms around her and holding her against his chest. His musk made her body tingle with desire. His warm breath fanned her ears. And she felt so good in his arms, like she was meant for him and him alone.

Akinyi was startled by his hold, not in a wrong way, the good kind of surprise. She even liked it too much. But her brain was warning her about all the negative consequences that could result from it.

She felt herself getting warm and turned on all at once. She had to get away before she threw all caution to the wind. She tried to pull away, but he did not let go. On second thought, she did not want to move. What harm was in letting herself be held? Such a simple pleasure.

"Relax, Akinyi, I don't bite," Adams whispered. He took her right ear into his warm mouth, nibbling as he caressed her belly.

She shifted, slipping out of his arms like she had been bitten, ready to leave.

This had not been a clever idea. It was still raining hard, and it would be foolish to walk home in the rain.

She quickly went to sit down, leaving Adams by the window, goading her. She poured a cup of tea.

He sat beside her after sweetening his tea.

"What is it about you that pulls me all in?" he asked, looking at her with no trace of his smile.

Her body stiffened, her mind ringing with alarm. He was a man in uniform, and they were all the same. They were not to be trusted.

"Never trust a man with a gun. He might blow your heart away," was her mantra.

He was going to leave just like David. She could not go through another breakup. She was still lost in her thoughts when Adams tipped her chin so that she could look at him.

Her gaze flew up immediately.

He stared at her mouth so greedily. His throat bobbed as he swallowed like it was some delicious meal that he wanted to savour for a long time.

She should move away from the single index finger holding her chin. Still, with his eyes riveted on hers, dark and desire-filled, she was helpless.

She thought he would kiss her and even closed her eyes in anticipation for a moment. Seconds later, she opened them to find him grinning like she was a joke from the Churchill show.

"I don't want anything to do with a man in uniform," she said tersely to cover her embarrassment.

"For a girl who has sworn off the men in uniform, you are doing a pretty good job," Adams said, chuckling under his breath, and the magic of the moment was blown away.

She quickly took her handbag from the chair and turned to leave. The rain had slowed down to a drizzle. He tugged at her hand, and she landed squarely on his lap.

"Let me go," she whimpered and hated herself the more. She was supposed to be demanding, not begging. But, with him this close and her butt on his muscular thighs, his hands circling her waist, and her heart beating so fast that he had to have heard it, it was impossible to be strong.

"Is that what you really want me to do?" Adams asked, kissing her and all reason flew out the window.

This was not fair. She had recently sworn off men, especially those in uniform and had no right feeling all the tingling from her head to her toes.

He stopped kissing her and stared at her for a reply. She didn't trust her voice to be steady, so she nodded.

"Alright, I guess I can take no for an answer," he said, putting her back on her feet.

She was supposed to feel relieved, but for some reason, she felt hot and bothered. He was playing with her libido, and just when she was soaring high like the eagle, he set her back on her feet. He stared with a smug grin.

Ahh! She felt like getting back at him.

She turned to face him and liked the surprised 'now what' expression on his face. She capitalised on it, moving closer until their bodies were just inches apart. She put his arms around his neck.

His eyes darkened with want. He pulled her into his body and lowered his mouth to hers. Sparks shot through her body as he groaned, deepening the kiss.

It had been long since she had been kissed like this. Not just the casual lip-locking but the thorough kissing that made her feel like she was knocking on Heaven's door.

CHAPTER THIRTEEN

Akinyi arrived at Grandma's house and found it packed with locals bearing different ailments—sprained wrists and ankles and snake bites.

The old woman was massaging a patient who had sprained the waist and was screaming like he was possessed.

"You are here just in time, Nyakwara. Boil that drug for me," she said, finishing with the patient.

Akinyi took the sufuria full of yellow leaves and went to the grass-thatched kitchen. When she returned, Grandma was sucking the venom from a child's leg. She spat it out, rubbed herbs into the wound and wrapped it with a piece of cloth. Then she instructed the child's mother to bring her the next day for a check-up.

The old woman continued attending to the patients for another hour.

"Thank you for your help," Grandma said, washing her hands. She was one of the few old people who could cure some diseases using herbs.

"My grandmother, the town healer," Akinyi said proudly.

She wondered about the graduates who tarmacked for jobs for several years, walking until their shoe soles got holes. Instead, her grandma, who had never stepped inside a classroom, earned a living using skills passed down to her by her mother.

"Pour some milk from that calabash," Grandma said, pointing at the calabash at the corner. Akinyi removed the maize cob lid and poured the milk into a cup after shaking the calabash. She tasted the milk and closed her eyes because the milk was sour. She was sure that her grandma had shaken it and left it to ferment for days.

"How is your mother?"

"She is fine. Where is Grandfather?"

"He is sleeping. You know, nowadays he usually sleeps from noon until the next day. So, tell me?"

"I want your opinion about cutting those trees. My mother says that it's blood money, and it was the reason for my father's death."

"Is that so?" Grandma asked, no doubt remembering her son. "I have heard that rumour going around too."

"But it's not true," Akinyi said firmly.

Grandma didn't respond, and she shook her head in disbelief. She had never understood why people always saw it fit to blame each other for the misfortune one was facing.

"I didn't expect this from you, too," she said, standing up and pacing the room.

"It is being rumoured. You know there can't be smoke without fire."

"No!"

"You have stirred enough problems with Ocholla. Let those trees be."

"So, I am a troublemaker?"

"I did not say that. After going to the university, you now think that our ways are barbaric."

"That's not true. I just want us to have a better life. My father worked hard planting those trees. So, we will let them be because if we cut them, someone might kill us."

"You see now. Don't disregard what you hear. You can always do what you deem right, but we have warned you," Grandma finally stood, indicating that the chapter was closed.

Akinyi was left staring at the wall. She had to do something.

***

Akinyi thought about the trees for another week. After so much deliberation, she decided to sell them. She quickly found a buyer willing to pay one thousand per tree and cut all the trees. This totalled around ten million shillings. She was so excited that she found herself turning all night long before D-day.

As the days went by, she found herself thinking less about David. Was time really the greatest healer, as they said? Or had she found better things that occupied her thoughts? She was tired of always looking at the past and regretting it. She had never imagined that David would move on without her. She could not have imagined a life without him, but she was alive and kicking.

When she informed her mother about her intention of selling the trees, her mother just sneered and kept quiet. Her Grandmother didn't even talk to her anymore; she just went about her chores ignoring her. She was tempted to let the tree be, but she didn't.

The following day, the timber yard personnel arrived, and they started cutting all the trees using the power saws. A crowd gathered at a distance, looking at everything in fascination. Finally, when all the trees had been loaded into the lorry, they handed her the cheque.

Her mother was looking at her keenly as she entered the house. "What is it, Mama?"

"Nothing, my daughter. I wondered how much our lives will cost," she said, still standing at the door.

Akinyi handed her the cheque and saw her eyes widen in awe. She was angry at her and Grandma for resisting this when it was the right thing to do. Her mother quickly put on a frown and handed her the cheque. She took it and walked into the house.

Her mother was still at the door, looking into thin air.

Akinyi knew her mother had loved Absalom very much. His life had more value than money. The stubborn woman would not allow herself to tarnish his memory by accepting the money.

***

Akinyi had decided to buy a water tank. Since her mother was still adamant about all this money, she wondered if she would also refuse to use anything purchased with the money. The locals were now gossiping about how rich she was. People kept coming to her house with different money problems—school fees, food and even a funeral. It was like she wanted to vie for the gubernatorial seat. She turned them away politely. She wasn't some charity organization.

"It's true that when you have money, everyone loves you," her mother commented one evening.

Her mother had thought about the issue and decided that too much tension brewed between them. While her daughter was always, she had worried they were going to die. But as the days turned into weeks, nothing happened. She then felt foolish for believing that Ochal would kill them with black magic as he had done to her Absalom.

"So, what are you planning to do with the money?"

"I wanted to buy a water tank," Akinyi said hesitantly.

"Only a water tank?"

"What is that supposed to mean? You didn't want the money. I am even starting to be frightened of spending it," she said, shifting in her seat.

"I am sorry about that. I know I should be an adult and be reasonable. I am afraid."

"But Mama, you can't live your life in constant fear of death. Everyone is going to die in the end."

"I know. I didn't want us to be killed because of that money. Our lives are more precious than money."

"They are, but that doesn't mean we should live half a life. Father worked hard to enable us to have this money. It can change our lives for the best."

Her mother nodded in understanding. She was then reminded that her daughter had grown into a wise woman. She was proud of her and knew that she and Absalom had done a wonderful job raising her.

She went to her mother and hugged her. They then started planning what they wanted to do around the house. Buy a tank, dig a well and build a new home. There was quite a lot to do.

***

On a warm July evening, Akinyi was busy cooking supper when Awino and her mother knocked at the door. She ushered them in.

Awino held her baby in her arms. Akinyi asked to carry the baby, and she handed it to her, adjusting the leso it was wrapped with. It was sleeping and looked peaceful.

"How are you feeling?" Akinyi asked.

"I am fine," Awino answered, looking at her mother.

Akinyi held the baby's hand, and she gripped it tightly, squirming and kicking her legs.

"Thank you again for everything. Awino insisted that we name the child after you," Awino's mother said.

"That is nice of you. When will Awino resume school?"

"I don't know. She has to look after the child for two years. I don't have time to sit at home and look after the child. I have to work," Awino's mother said, looking downcast.

Akinyi wanted to tell her that Awino needed to be in school but changed her mind. Their family needed food to eat, and therefore Awino's mother could not afford to stay at home.

"That's unfortunate. Two years is a long time. Let me think about it and see how we can handle the situation better."

"Thank you. When you come up with something, let me know."

"I will," Akinyi said, handing the baby to Awino. After they left, an idea came to her. Adams had finished building his home, but Akinyi doubted whether he could mop the house on his own and run the other household chores.

When she asked him about it, he quickly agreed that Mama Awino could help him with the household chores. Mama Awino was happy about the arrangement. She stated that she was tired of working on people's farms, plus the salary was enough to fend for her children. She, therefore, was going to look after her granddaughter while Awino resumed school in the next year.

CHAPTER FOURTEEN

Akinyi went to Grandma's house after washing the clothes. She found her grandma with a patient, a young woman of about thirty years. After greeting them, she took her seat.

"What are you ailing from?" Grandma asked the patient.

"My heart has collapsed. I can't feel it."

"Ooh. You have to plant a banana tree. As the banana grows, your heart will grow with it."

The patient nodded, smiling and left after giving her grandma money. Akinyi shook her head in disbelief, wondering how someone could still walk with a collapsed heart.

"Grandma, how are you?" she asked.

"I am fine. You haven't come to visit in a long while."

"You didn't seem to want to talk to me."

"It's because you were being stubborn. You went ahead and cut the trees anyway."

"Are you still angry at me?"

"No, I have been thinking about it, and I hate to admit that you were right. We should pray for God's protection always."

Akinyi didn't speak for a while. Grandma stood up, went into the cupboard, and brought boiled groundnuts in a metallic bowl. They ate it in silence.

"Grandma, during your time, what usually happened to those who defiled their children?"

Grandma smiled, and the wrinkles on her face deepened. "We didn't have so many cases then. It was an abomination. Whoever did that would be excommunicated, ridiculed by the villagers, sent away from the village, or sometimes even stoned to death. Why do you ask?"

"I have heard some disturbing rumours at Agawo si Kenya. Men sleeping with their children, old men inheriting a series of widows and the women luring the boys."

Grandma hummed to herself shaking her head. "The society is in a drunken stupor. The chief is supposed to be at the forefront, punishing all the offenders. But you know our people say that the snake has entered a calabash. They protect the perpetrators."

"But I haven't heard of such stories in Kakelo, yet it is just our neighbour."

"That is because the Kakelo people live by different principles; they are quick with pangas. Anyone who commits such an offence is slashed to death. Hence nobody would dare. The chief is also keen on the education of children."

"Then why don't Kachieng' people do the same."

Grandma chewed on her groundnut, obviously pondering the statement. "I wonder what is happening to this town. The old men who are supposed to sit in barazas and talk about it are the perpetrators. It is time for someone to shake the town from its slumber," Grandma said, looking at her.

Akinyi stared back at her, not believing what she was insinuating. "You have to help the young girls and boys in this town, the way you helped Awino. It takes a strong person to be brave in the face of adversity. You can do it."

She was still reeling from everything that Grandma was saying. "Grandma, I don't think I want to go through a scenario like the Ocholla sons. I almost died."

"I know you are scared. But, you don't have to do it alone. You can get people to help you like the government."

Akinyi looked at Grandma's bright face and saw her optimism and belief in her. This was going to necessitate the establishment of an organization to fight for children's rights. She did the maths and knew that it would need a lot of money. But she again remembered that money was not a problem now. She could use the money from the trees. She could also write proposals to get donors who could fund the project. This was all very possible!

"Ooh, Grandma, thank you very much," she said, squeezing her hand.

"You are always welcome, Nyakwara."

The better part of the night she spent thinking about the project, the possible name, and the staff she was to employ. She shared the plans with her mother, who was supportive. She was extremely excited about the project.

She decided to call it Kachieng Child's Right Organisation. She was hesitant about inviting Adhiambo to become one of the staff. However, when she called, she was surprised.

"How are you? I have really missed you."

"I have missed you too, Adhiambo. I miss our walks to Abururu."

"Me too. How is the Prado man?"

"He is fine. Are you really alright? Your voice sounds like you have been crying or having a cold."

"I am fine. I just miss home," Adhiambo said, now sobbing loudly.

"What is wrong? Please talk to me."

"Ooh, Akinyi. This man is terrible. I wonder how my sister used to live with him."

"What has he done?"

"He rarely sleeps at home. I have heard that he has inherited two widows. He drinks and smokes. He also beats me..." she said between sobs, and Akinyi felt her heart crack.

"I am so sorry," Akinyi consoled her.

Adhiambo broke into a loud cry, making tears cloud her eyes. She forced them back. She was supposed to be consoling her, not crying.

"Everything will be fine. You will see."

"No, it won't. I have only stayed here for three months. I think it's going to get worse with time."

Akinyi was quiet for a while. She didn't know what to say.

"I am coming home. I would rather die an old maid."

"Will he allow you to leave?"

"I don't know. It is not up to him. I will sneak if I have to," Adhiambo said, sniffing.

"I am sorry, my friend. I will see you when you get home then." Adhiambo agreed, and they ended the phone call.

Akinyi sat in a daze long afterwards.

Adhiambo returned two days later and visited Akinyi's house, limping slightly. Her face was covered in bruises.

"Ooh, Akinyi," she whispered as they hugged.

After sitting down, Adhiambo narrated all she had gone through. Akinyi felt both angry and sad.

"Why didn't his mother do anything when he beat you? Did you shout for help?"

"I don't know. All the while, she was out washing her utensils like it was normal. I later went to her to report the beating. Guess what she did?"

Akinyi shook her head, and she continued, "She showed me her missing thumb and told me that her husband had cut it and never once did she leave. This only meant that my beatings were trivial and were a way of the husband showing his love to the wife."

"I am sorry. How did you manage to leave?"

"I sneaked when they went to the market. All that matters now is that I am here. What did you want to talk to me about anyway?"

"I am opening an office to help children fight for their rights. I want you to be my assistant," Akinyi told her.

"But I don't have any college degree or experience for this sort of thing," Adhiambo said hesitantly.

"Don't worry about that. I will show you what to do. We can even work out a way for you to enrol for a Community Development Course at Sikri Technical College."

"Really? Will you pay me?"

"Of course, you won't be working for free."

"I can't wait to begin. Thank you very much," Adhiambo said gleefully.

CHAPTER FIFTEEN

Akinyi noticed that her mother was losing weight. She had become restless and slept for longer hours.

"Mama, how are you feeling?" Akinyi asked.

Her mother sat on a stool, washing clothes. She had never seen her mother do her chores while seated.

"I am fine. I am only tired. I think I am getting old. Look at you now, a full-grown woman." She motioned at her daughter.

Akinyi smiled before asking, "I think you are unwell. Your clothes loosely fit, and your complexion is darker."

"I don't know, my daughter. Maybe your uncle has visited that ajuoga, and they plan on killing me. Yesterday some Legion Maria passed by and told me that he could see that someone had my heart in a bottle."

"Mama, please stop all this witchcraft stuff!"

"I told you they were going to kill us over those trees. You are so stubborn like your father. You never listen to anything I say."

"Nobody is going to die, Mama. God will protect us," Akinyi said, looking at her mother and daring her to say otherwise.

Her mother stopped washing and looked at the horizon where the sun was setting. Then, her mother started coughing incessantly.

Akinyi rushed to her side, rubbing her back. "Ooh, Mama. Let's go to the house. You need to lie down."

On the way to the house, her mother began vomiting.

Akinyi felt her insides churn when she saw traces of blood. She helped her mother to a stool, but the coughing didn't stop for a while. Then, she retrieved her phone and dialled Adams' number.

It took Adams five minutes to get to the house. By then, her mother was lying on the sofa. They helped her to the car and drove to Rachuonyo SubCounty hospital. They found long queues and bossy nurses who weren't in a hurry to attend to them. Adams walked to one of the nurses, and after some time, her mother was wheeled into the doctor's office.

They had to wait out as the doctors ran tests on her. Akinyi felt her fear mounting with every passing minute. Her mind was visiting the worst possible scenarios. What if her mother had some incurable disease? What if she was dead already?

"Jaber, stop overthinking," he said, taking her hand.

"I can't. Why is this happening to us? She was healthy," she said, tears filling her eyes.

"Hush. We will know for sure when the doctor comes out."

Akinyi wiped her tears and asked, "What did you tell the nurse to convince her to attend us?"

"I told her that she was beautiful and winked at her," he said smoothly.

Akinyi laughed and said, "You are kidding, right?"

"No, I am not. Every woman likes to be appreciated by a handsome man. Have you seen me?" he asked, pointing at his face.

"Mr Arrogant," she said, suppressing her laughter.

The doctor's door opened, and Akinyi stood up and rushed in. Adams wanted to give them privacy, so he remained out.

The doctor motioned for Akinyi to take a seat. After sitting down, the doctor cleared his voice, "How are you?"

"I am fine. How is my mother?"

The doctor didn't answer immediately. He stared into her eyes, drumming his fingers on the wooden table. Akinyi felt like she was almost snapping, sitting at the edge of her seat.

"I am sorry. The patient has Stage 4 Stomach Cancer."

She gasped and felt the room whirling like she was on a merry go round. Cancer? This couldn't be. Her mother had been eating healthy food. Where did the disease come from? An illness with no cure! The chemotherapy was just a way of prolonging life. Her mother was surely going to die. She felt so empty and hollow. Why was life so unfair?

The doctor cleared his voice tugging her from her thoughts. "How far has it spread?" she asked in a dreamlike voice.

"It has spread to the kidney, pancreas, liver, and intestines," the doctor said apologetically.

Was this the end of the road for her mother? She suspected it was just a matter of time before cancer spread to the heart, hushing it forever.

The doctor explained that they had to transfer her to Jaramogi Oginga Odinga Teaching and Referral Hospital for chemotherapy.

She walked out of the room in a daze, more like a zombie. Adams looked up from his phone and went to her. She was so pale, sad, and distant. He hugged her tightly, and she let herself go. The tears came, but he didn't let go. Akinyi fainted after that and couldn't really remember what happened later.

She woke up at home, and it was dark. At first, she thought she had been dreaming, but a walk into the empty bedroom told her that it was all real. She found Grandma in the sitting room. She began crying again, and Grandma consoled her.

***

Akinyi looked at her mother's frail figure on the bed and wept. She was wasting away like a wilting flower, and the doctors had lost hope, now counting her days. She'd been given two months to live.

Akinyi could not imagine how her life would turn out without her. She had come to depend on her so much. She was afraid of losing her. First, her father had left her, then David and now her mother. How much more was she going to lose before she could gain?

Akinyi was still deep in her thoughts when she heard her mother groaning in pain.

"Akinyi, my daughter, I have one favour to ask from you before I join your father," she said in a whisper as she coughed incessantly.

Akinyi held her thin hands and said, "Anything you want, Mama."

"Would you please get married while I am still alive? I want to ensure that your father's generation doesn't fizzle out. I am asking a lot. Please forgive me," her mother pleaded.

Akinyi almost screamed in protest, but one look into her mother's sunken eyes, and she knew that would surely kill her.

"Alright, Mama. I will," Akinyi said in an assuring tone, while deep inside, she knew all was not well.

"Thank you very much, my daughter. Please don't tell your grandmother about this. I know she won't approve." Her mother coughed.

Akinyi assured her that it would be a secret, and her mother drifted off to sleep, leaving her battling with her thoughts. Where would she get a husband to marry her in less than two months? She did not want to get married that soon. She still had a lot of things to do before settling down.

She was tempted to call David. But since he hadn't contacted her despite the numerous messages she left him, she didn't feel right about calling him. It was going to come off as desperate. She had to still hold her head high.

She then thought of Adams and felt a slight shiver from her head to her toes.

Adams made her come alive. He always looked at her with those bedroom eyes like she was the most prized treasure on earth. His touches had slowly inched down her face like she was a fragile glass and had to be handled with care. She had never felt anything like that with David. Maybe good things fell apart so that better things could fall together.

CHAPTER SIXTEEN

Adams was in the bathroom when she arrived. She wondered what it would be like to share his shower.

When Adams cleared his voice at the door, Akinyi looked at him from a whole new perspective, and she wondered what it would feel like to share his house for a short while.

"What a pleasant surprise! I was beginning to think that you had forgotten all about me," Adams said, entering the sitting room. He smelt of soap, his aftershave and his sweet natural scent that she had come to associate with only him. His white shirt and blue thigh hugging jeans made Akinyi feast her eyes on him until he got to his seat. She could not just help it. Something innate was driving her to him, something beyond her control.

"This is awkward, but I have to ask," Akinyi said, looking into his eyes to gauge his mood.

"Go ahead," Adams urged her.

She plucked up her courage and asked, "My mother's last dying wish is that I should get a husband. I have explored all my options, and I think you are my best bet." She finished and felt all too tired and relieved at the same time. However, she was worried when Adams frowned and shifted uncomfortably in his seat.

"Let me get this right. You want me to be your husband. You wanted nothing to do with me because I was once a man in uniform. What has changed?" Adams asked.

"It is only in name," she quickly assured him. "After she dies, we can go back to being friends."

"What is the difference? The fact is that I was once a man in uniform, and you despise the men in uniform. You keep running hot and cold on me. What has changed?"

Akinyi could not form an answer immediately. She did not want a man in uniform. No change there. She just wanted a temporary marriage that would appease her mother. She looked into Adams' eyes and saw all the longing in them as he bathed her in his gaze. Then, she knew there would be nothing temporary about their marriage.

"Nothing has changed," Akinyi stated and got off her seat. She was angry, but she did not know why. She had expected too much from him, just as she always did. She knew first-hand how too many expectations often lead to disappointment.

"Goodbye, Adams," she said and felt tears forming in her eyes and turned sharply to leave.

At the door, Adams grabbed the knob before her. He saw the tears in her eyes, cursed under his breath and took her into his arms, holding her tightly.

Akinyi sobbed quietly into his shirt. After calming, she pulled away from him.

He tugged her back to him and crushed her mouth with his.

Confused, she took a while to respond to the kiss. He deepened the kiss, and she had no option but to respond with the same energy.

He explored her mouth with his tongue, groaning. Shivering, she put her hands around his neck and moved closer. He moaned deep in his throat, and her inner princess danced around the room, ululating triumphantly.

She had never been kissed with such passion and abandon. She broke the kiss, shifting so she could look into his eyes.

He stared at her and smiled before kissing her tears away. She felt warm with every kiss, and when he finally pressed his lips to her eyes so tenderly, she knew her time was up.

He cupped her face in his hands, looked deep into her eyes, and said, "Damn it, Akinyi! Don't ever cry on me!"

He brushed her nose with his. They stayed that way for a while, their heartbeat and breathing the only sounds in the room.

"I cannot marry you in name only. I want you so much. The whole of you. I wonder what the men in uniform ever did to you, but I assure you I am different," Adams said.

She saw the sincerity in his eyes, but David had also shown such sincerity and still broken her heart.

"I cannot take that chance," she said, turning on her heels to leave.

It was dusk, so she rushed home before it became darker. She felt so alone, despair eating away at her. Feeling cold, she hugged her sweater closer to her body. When she finally got home, her head ached from thinking and deliberating.

She checked on her mother and found that she was still sleeping. The nurse informed her that she had eaten just ten minutes ago. Akinyi herself did not feel like eating. She took some painkillers and retired to bed.

***

After Akinyi had left, Adams felt a heaviness weighing so strong in his heart. He was tempted to follow her but resisted the urge.

Why did saying no to her request feel so wrong when it was the right call? He paced about the living room. He knew that he was hooked. He hadn't planned on falling in love or whatever they call these strange feelings that engulf you and force you to bow to their will. But, with her, he wanted nothing less than to belong to her and her to him.

He sat down and tried to watch some news to get his mind off her, but it was pointless. Then it hit him that since he had turned down her offer of marriage, she would choose another man for the role.

Who knew, the arrangement might turn out to be permanent. Hence he would surely lose her for good. He shrugged and told himself that it didn't matter. But deep down, he knew that he cared more than he dared admit to himself.

He pictured another man laying his hands on her—touching, kissing her and making love to her like he'd wanted since they first met. He bolted off the chair like it had become too hot. That could not be! He had to be the one doing all those things to her. He quickly looked at his watch and rushed to pick up his keys from the counter. He had to see her, and it could not wait until the next day.

When he arrived at her house, it was around 8pm. The maid opened the door for him. He went to see Akinyi's mother in her room and found her wide awake. She looked at him disinterestedly as she drifted off to sleep. He sat on the stool next to the bed and held her thin, frail hands that were warm.

"I want to marry your daughter," Adams said, surprising himself since the words were alien even to his ears, yet the voice was his. What had come over him? He had never felt this strange feeling that pushed him to do right by any woman not related to him by blood. Akinyi's mother's eyes flew open, and her face broke into a smile that made her face light up.

"Thank you, my son. Now I can rest in peace knowing that she is in safe hands," she said and closed her eyes.

Adams went in search of Akinyi and found her fast asleep. He had intended to wake her and tell her the good news but changed his mind. She looked too peaceful to be disturbed. So he went to her, kissed her goodnight on the forehead and left.

***

The following day Akinyi woke up late, but she was still feeling very exhausted. She yawned, stretched, and got out of bed. She went to her mother's room and found her awake already with a big smile plastered on her face.

"Mama, you are very bright today. That's lovely," Akinyi said jubilantly.

"Yes, my daughter. I have never been better," her mother answered, her smile intriguing.

"What aren't you telling me, Mama?" Akinyi asked, eyeing her suspiciously.

"Don't lie to me. You already know," her mother insisted.

"No. I would also be brimming with joy if I knew," Akinyi said, the suspense killing her.

"Alright. The young man, Adams Okal, came to ask for your hand in marriage. That boy is God-sent, isn't he?" her mother said.

Akinyi's slight smile turned into a frown. What had made him change his mind? Last night he had been adamant about marrying her. She had really wanted him to say yes, but now that he had, she did not know what to feel.

"What's wrong? I thought you would be jumping with joy by now," her mother asked.

Akinyi smiled. "I am happy, Mama. It's just that I didn't expect him to say yes that fast."

The news made her mother happy because it was what she really wanted. On the other hand, Akinyi had not planned on getting married in the foreseeable future. But she did not have a choice in the matter. It just had to be done.

She bathed her mother, and after feeding her, she left for Adam's house. It was then that the news really dawned on her. Adams was going to be her husband. Even though it was in name only, she feared the unknown. If seeing him occasionally was

113

too much to handle, how about staying with him under the same roof?

She walked to the front door timidly and rang the alarm. Mama Awino rushed to open the door and welcome her into the house. She asked about Awino and her baby before inquiring about Adams.

"He is in the study room," the woman commented.

She went to the study, glancing at the other room, all spotlessly clean. She knocked on the door slightly before entering.

He sat at the desk, reading. Dressed in a blue shirt and a pair of black jeans, he looked handsome. He lifted his head, his brown eyes flicking over her, undressing her.

Adams thanked his lucky stars for bringing him to Kachieng. Akinyi was in a white floral dress clinging in all the right places. Her big eyes looked back at him defiantly. It was rare to find beauty and brains in a woman. He had been troubled all night that he had made a rash decision, but seeing her looking so beautiful in front of him, he knew she was meant for him. He closed his books and set them aside.

"Good morning, Jaber. Have a seat," Adams said, extending his hand.

She took it, sitting beside him. There was a tense and awkward silence about the room.

"Akinyi, I came to your house last night and asked for your hand in marriage," Adams said, resuming his seat. Akinyi forced her eyes to move from his lips to his eyes.

"Why the sudden change of heart? Is it out of pity?" Akinyi asked, trying to regain her composure. What was wrong with her? She didn't know why being around him always made her have wayward thoughts.

And Adams chuckled before saying, "I feel many things for you, Akinyi, but pity is not one of them."

Curiosity took the better part of her, and she asked, "What are these things that you feel for me, Adams?"

He liked how she called out his name, like a plea.

"Right now, I feel like taking you across my lap and kissing you senselessly." He laughed loudly when he saw how Akinyi's eyes widened in surprise.

"You are crazy, I swear," she said, smiling.

"Maybe, but I am used to saying what is on my mind. I always get what I want, Akinyi, always." Adams appraised her body until his eyes rested on hers.

She felt heat rising to her face and quickly looked away and murmured, "So domineering."

He stood up from his seat, and all her senses became so alert. Was he going to act on his word? For a strange reason, Akinyi wished he would kiss her. But he strode purposefully to the home theatre radio occupying one corner of the room and switched on the music. Disappointment washed over Akinyi. He was such a tease.

The refined sound of Johnny Junior's song of 'Adongo' filled the room. Then, he walked back to her and held out his hand. Akinyi blinked in surprise. This man was very unpredictable.

"I don't know how to dance," she whispered because she had lost her voice.

"I will lead, and you follow," he explained, and she put her hand in his and stood up. He held the small of her back and pulled her to him, and they started swaying to the music.

She felt so tense being this close to him at the beginning. She felt his body heat permeating through his shirt to her skin. She looked up at him and found him smiling down at her. His bald head and his grown beards made him look dangerous and handsome. She lifted her right hand and gently caressed his beard, liking their coarse feel in her hands.

He closed his eyes and inhaled deeply. They were bright when he opened them, with purposeful light added to them. She knew then that she was playing with fire, and she would soon get burnt.

As the music went on, she relaxed and leaned her head at the crook of his neck, liking the smell of his skin and his beards tickling her cheeks. When he felt her breathing on his neck, he tightened his hold on her, and she felt so protected, so possessed, like she belonged to him. She wanted to remain like this forever and feel only him. True to his word, he was leading, and she would follow wherever he went.

He cupped her face in his hands, placed his lips on hers, and kissed her so slowly, gently, and deeply that she felt tears coming to her eyes. She had never felt such a profound connection with any man. Then, he pulled from the kiss, and she saw his eyes darken with something akin to lust. She wanted to look away but could not. She felt a tremor run through her.

"Are you cold?" he asked, running his hands up and down her arm. No, just feeling like taking this beyond the study room, she almost said but couldn't find the courage to do so.

Akinyi pulled from his arms and sat down. "Let us make this marriage a temporary deal. Just until my mother ... dies," she said, almost afraid to spell out the last word.

Adams looked at her as if she had suddenly grown horns on her head.

"What? You thought it would be a permanent arrangement?" she asked.

"Not at all. Temporary is good enough but don't you think it should be negotiable. For example, if you find that you love me after staying together, we can prolong it," he inquired.

He wanted to make her so happy that she wouldn't want to leave his side when her mother died. He was going to give it his all.

"I doubt whether I will ever fall in love again, Adams. Mine is a lost case," she said in a wistful tone that pierced his heart.

"What did that man do to you? Not all men in uniform are dogs. Furthermore, remember, I have retired from the forces," he pleaded for understanding.

She knew that there were men in the forces who were honourable, sensible, and responsible like Adams. All he had shown her was love and kindness, but the hurt had cut deep, leaving her slow to trust again. She was still walking around like some wounded animal, and she wondered just for a second if she was letting the past hurt and disappointments shadow the present. She wished she could wake up one day and realize that she had selective amnesia and could not remember the past hurts. She really wanted to give the present a shot. They said that time heals all wounds; she just hoped they would heal sooner.

CHAPTER SEVENTEEN

"How about some ground rules? Would you expect me to cook for you, wash your clothes?" Akinyi asked as they strolled to the house.

"Mama Awino can do all that, but I will appreciate the effort if you want to do them," Adams said, enjoying the smile on her face. She didn't like housework, he concluded. He did not expect her to look after him.

Thoughts of how she had laboured for David, hoping he would marry her, rushed forth. Cooking for him, washing and ironing his clothes and cleaning the house on fours to ensure it was spotlessly clean. She had been so foolish, but not anymore. She remembered how they had browsed the internet with Ephy on 'how to please a man.' They had even listened to Bi Mswafari's advice on Citizen TV on being a good wife. Read the proverbs about the virtuous woman. When a woman wants to get married, she'd do anything for a man.

"How about the sleeping arrangements?" she asked.

"What about them, Akinyi?" he asked, and she had to blush.

"I want my own room," she said, expecting him to protest. Still, his firm composure gave nothing away about his feelings concerning the suggestion.

"So, you will have your room," he said. He wouldn't have minded being her bedfellow, but her wish was his command. "Don't worry, I won't take the fake conjugal rights using force. I like my women compliant."

She gave him the once over and knew that most women wouldn't mind sharing his bed. The thought made her feel a twinge of jealousy. Men like him could not wait around or chase a woman that long.

If it didn't come soon, he would find his amusement in the arms of other women.

Akinyi swore to herself and God that she was never giving sex to receive love again. Love and sex came from separate places. She had learnt her bitter lessons the hard way.

She wanted to suggest impossible rules so that he could bolt. However, he showed no sign of backing down, and she knew that pleasing her meant something to him. Why did it make her heart warm up even more towards him?

"Can I bring my cat too?" she asked, and the frown marring his handsome face told her she was pushing too hard.

"Don't you think you are milking me dry as it is?" he asked, and she just shrugged, batting her lashes.

The way she stared at him made him want to do anything for her, including climbing Mt. Kenya and swimming across Lake Victoria.

Separate bedrooms he could condone but adding a cat on top of that was just pure torture. The cat would be invited into her room, but it was out of bounds for him. She was so unfair. He was never a fan of cats since childhood. He was keen on dogs, but he had never entertained the idea of owning those squirming balls of warmth and fur.

"On the condition that the cat doesn't interfere with my personal space. Plus, you should not allow it in your bed because the fur can cause serious respiratory problems," he ordered.

"Yes, sir," she answered, and he smiled.

Old habits died hard. He was so used to spelling out orders and commands.

"Let me take you to your room," he said, already leading the way, and she duly followed him. Something was intriguing about a man in uniform that she could not resist. His broad back and muscular thighs exuded power and confidence about him. When they reached the room, she almost bumped into him because her eyes were on his beautiful back and her thoughts very occupied.

"Watch where you are going, Sexy Back," he said, steadying her, and she mumbled an apology. She mused that he was the one with the sexy back, not her.

"Why are you calling me Sexy Back?" she asked.

"Come, I'll show you," he said, pulling her into the room to the front of a huge mirror occupying one wall. He told her to turn around so that they could inspect her backside together. She did as she was told, blushing from head to toe. He traced her back with his hands like he sculptured her, and she went all still. When he came to the small of her back, his hands paused for some seconds before he cupped her buttocks in his two hands and pulled her hard against his hard-muscled body. Taken by surprise, she gasped, trying to hold his bulging biceps for support. He grinned and freed her, leaving her so bereft.

"This is your room," he announced after a while. Akinyi looked at him like he was speaking Kikamba. How could he manage to move from one steamy moment and be all official the next? She nodded to clear it and looked about the room for the first time since entering it.

The bed was king-size with pink sheets with white flowers and a matching pair of pillows. The bed was well spread that she felt like hopping into it and sleeping forever. The walls were painted pink, and the floor tiles were cotton white.

There was also a walk-in closet where she would hang her clothes and a small oval table with a mirror in front of it. This was where she was going to be applying her makeup.

OMG, she had been Plain Jane, only applying some powder and lip-gloss. Not to mention the variety of designer perfumes on the dresser. She inhaled each one of them before settling on a mild one.

He watched her as she looked around the room and knew she liked it from the way her eyes lit as they noticed the room's details. He led her to the bathroom. There was a white bathtub occupying most of the room. There was a cupboard containing a variety of bathing soaps, very thick candles, and a small speaker on the top of the dresser. She could already visualize herself in the bathtub covered with soapy water with her head resting in one corner of the bathtub. She also saw lit candles surrounding the bathtub with classical blues playing in the background. But she imagined that adding Adams to the picture would make the picture complete, picture-perfect.

As much as she was fighting it, she knew that he was starting to pull some of her heartstrings, and she hoped that in future, her heart could sing the song of love, just maybe. She was afraid of letting down her guards. But what use are walls when they make you a prisoner?

***

Akinyi visited Grandma and found her preparing supper in the smoke-filled kitchen. Akinyi fanned the smoke that was now making her eyes and nose water, and Grandma shook her head, smiling. She helped her carry the food back to the house.

"I wonder why you don't want me to buy you a gas cooker. It cooks faster and has no trace of smoke," Akinyi reminded her again, but Grandma dismissed her with a wave of her hand.

"You have done enough already. You have changed my roof and plastered the whole house. Besides, I like cooking on the three stones. I have done it ever since I was a little girl."

"But Grandma, you should try the gas cooker."

Grandma shook her head, "Forgive me, but this is enough change. You can call me old fashioned, but when you get to my age, you want predictability and familiarity."

"Alright, Grandma, at least I tried," Akinyi said not so happily.

"Don't look like a cat that has been rained on. Do you know that we used to even grind our own maize using stone in my days?"

"Really? How was that even possible?"

"We would put the maize on a big flat stone and use a smaller one to grind it—"

"How long would that take?" Akinyi asked, interrupting.

"Long enough, it wasn't optional. There were no posho mills. It was the first thing every newly married woman was taught."

"Then marriage was a serious business back then."

"It was. The first test was to cook ugali for the whole clan. This proved how well the woman was equipped to care for the husband."

Akinyi laughed, and her grandma grinned before going on, "Most of the people in your generation go into marriage not knowing their roles and responsibilities. Marriage is called katedo, which loosely translates to cooking. Some go into marriage without even the slightest idea of preparing tea."

"Grandma, you can't blame us for that. We spend most of the time in school. Therefore, we have no time to learn how to cook."

Grandma snorted before saying, "No time for even the basics? That is just laziness on the parents and the children."

Akinyi shrugged and said, "Most women today have to go to work. Hence the maids take up most of the workload."

Grandma shook her head vigorously and said, "That is no excuse for a woman to neglect her roles. Remember, first, you are a wife and a mother before a worker. Let the maid do the chores concerning the child. Cooking and washing your husband's clothes are your sole role. That's why he married you."

Akinyi saw how serious Grandma's face was and knew this was not a laughing matter.

"Some women still wonder what their husbands see in house-helps. You let the maid run your house. Cooking your husband's food, washing his clothes, and even making your bed," she said the last statement in disgust.

Akinyi broke into laughter.

"This is not a laughing matter, Nyakwara," Grandma said, grinning.

"Another thing you should know is that you need to respect your in-laws. Some in-laws can get difficult, but you must just learn how to cope with them, especially the mother-in-law."

"But most mothers-in-law are hell, Grandma."

"I know. Some feel insecure that their sons will stop buying them food and other responsibilities. So they see you as their competitor."

Akinyi wondered how difficult such a life would be. Why was it always the woman who had to leave her people to join the man's family?

"So, what do you suppose I should do when my mother-in-law lashes out insults at me?"

"You should just ignore her. Eventually, she will get tired and respect you for it. Don't ever insult her the way I see some women standing outside their houses with their hands akimbo throwing insults like arrows."

"But marriage sounds so difficult and complicated," Akinyi complained.

"It is not a bed of roses. But it has its good side. You will get companionship from your husband, and you will be proud when you walk among your peers. The pride of a woman is to get married. You will get children too."

Akinyi considered the good side. "It's not that bad. What is your opinion on the men who beat their wives?"

"A man shows his love by beating the woman. If your man does not beat you, then he does not love you."

Akinyi stifled a laugh before asking, "There are a thousand ways to show love. Why would my husband beat me?"

"I am not talking about the beating where men cut off their wives' hands or even hack them to death. Like your grandfather used to tell us, all the eight wives, to lie down on our stomachs. He would then cane us if one of the women made a mistake."

"That can't be true, grown women lying down like some primary school pupils. Why did you let him do that?"

"We didn't consider it wrong. It was his way of disciplining us. Plus, he would ask where you were when your co-wife erred. We, therefore, had to look out for each other if we didn't want to get in trouble."

Akinyi shook her head in disbelief. "I don't think I would like my husband to discipline me that way. We should just sit down like grownups and solve our issues."

Grandma nodded and said, "If that works for you. By the way, after the caning, my behind would swell and ache until the next day."

They both laughed at the memory.

"And you would still cook for him?"

"Of course, that is my role. His hut was at the centre of the homestead. It was called Abila. After cooking, every woman was to take food to the abila."

Akinyi looked at Grandma, bemused. "I still wonder why you would get married as the fifth wife. You could have had your own husband."

"Back then, marrying many wives was the norm. Not like today when there are so many diseases like HIV. I didn't mind as long as the man had enough wealth to provide for the family."

"Ooh, Grandma. How did you meet?"

"Your grandpa came to do some work in my village. He was a tractor driver then and lived in the nearby market centre. I usually took him milk since we had dairy cows. He was the most handsome man I had ever seen. He wooed me, and when it was his time to leave, he asked me to marry him."

"And you said yes? Did he tell you that he already had four wives?"

"He told me about the wives, but I loved him too much to let that deter me. My father also had three wives, and the idea wasn't that alien. He took twenty heads of cows to my father as dowry."

Grandma recalled the younger years with nostalgia, eyes lit up.

Akinyi wondered what love had meant in those days. Could a man love different women equally?

"By the way, I came to inform you that I am getting married to Mr Okal," Akinyi said and wished Grandma wouldn't read into her thoughts.

"Wonderful. He is such a fine young man; polite, respectful, hardworking," she said, folding her fingers, ticking off the qualities.

"Have you met his people?"

"No."

"And you are going to marry him, just like that. The people of this generation never fail to amuse me."

"But I love him," Akinyi said, trying to convince her.

Her Grandma shook her head violently and sneered. "Love. What is love? When you marry a man, you marry his whole clan. You must find out beforehand the kind of people they are. What if he is a wizard? Or have some of the illnesses like albinism? What if the clan is cursed?"

"Sorry, Grandma. I hadn't thought of all that."

"You should. Where is his home? Why did he decide to leave his home and set up here? Are his parents still alive? Does he have any siblings?"

"I haven't really enquired about those."

"Then what do you talk about? Those are basic questions that you should know about the person you are planning to spend the rest of your life with," Grandma said, her voice rising.

"Alright, Grandma. I will enquire about all those things."

"You should. Marriage is a lifelong commitment."

Akinyi was tempted to bare her soul and reveal that it was a temporary arrangement but couldn't find the courage to betray her mother's trust.

CHAPTER EIGHTEEN

Akinyi rearranged her room, checking that she had brought everything. Eventually, she opened the doors to the closet, and her mouth fell agape.

Beautiful dresses hung in it, most of them in shades of purple.

Adams had taken notice of her favourite colour. There was nothing she loved more than keenness in a man.

The shoe rack had six different shoes—two heeled, three sandals and a pair of flat-heeled pumps.

She tried them, and they fit neatly. Excited, she grabbed one of the dresses and found a handwritten note attached to it, handwritten.

I couldn't receive you but feel most welcome. I hope you like everything. See you at 8 pm for supper.

She held the note close to her heart and couldn't help going through it again.

By the time everything was in its rightful place, she was very exhausted. She lay on the bed to rest, closing her eyes.

The squeaking sound of the door jolted her awake. She sat up reluctantly, rubbing her eyes.

Adams leaned on the door with his hands in his pocket, eyeing her keenly.

"You either come in or go out, Mr Adams Okal." She smiled, and he walked across the room.

"Do you know that you snore like a trailer, Sexy Back?" he said, sitting on the bed.

"No way. I sleep quietly like a baby," she countered.

"Where is that cat you were talking about?" he asked, surveying the place.

"There is no cat. I was just toying with you."

"Thank God. Have you eaten supper?" he asked, and she shook her head.

"I'm too tired to eat. Maybe tomorrow." She stifled a third yawn in two minutes.

"You can't go to bed hungry. Let's eat. I prefer my women fleshy." He reached out, holding her hand already.

My women? He had the audacity to mention other women in her presence? How mannerless could a man get?

She wanted to reprimand him, then remembered the marriage was supposed to be a fake. She wasn't supposed to take things so seriously, yet it was still unsettling.

When they got to the dining room, the table was already set, and they sat down to eat. The meal consisted of grilled beef, sukuma wiki and ugali. It smelled heavenly, and the taste was even better. Mama Awino could really cook.

She looked at him across the table and found him eyeing her. "What?"

He just chuckled. "It's just that I am so taken by your beauty. I can't help but stare."

She blushed. The man knew just what to say, didn't he?

She suddenly lost her appetite for food, developing a craving for other things she couldn't dare say. She started picking out the tomatoes from her food.

"Eat your food unless you want me to feed you like a small baby," he warned.

"Do you know how old I am? I'm past being fed," she retorted with a smile.

"Of course, no one can convince me you're a baby with a body like yours." He grinned, staring at her body approvingly, lingering a little longer on her breasts.

As if on cue, her nipples hardened beneath her dress. How would she survive for a long while pretending to be his wife?

When his eyes lifted to meet hers, they were hot with desire, shamelessly revealing the direction of his wayward thoughts.

After quickly gobbling the rest of the now cold food, she pushed back her chair and went to the bathroom.

Akinyi dried her body after the bath and applied lotion. She felt so fresh and rejuvenated. All the while, her mind was on Adams.

He was so kind, so patient, and so handsome. She couldn't help wanting to spend more time with him. Her body was willing, but her heart and mind were resisting.

She had to see her mother early in the morning, so she went to bed. She still had time to ponder on her decision.

***

"Goodnight, Adams, see you tomorrow," Akinyi said and rushed off to her room before Adams could even reply.

Was she scared of him?

In contrast, he was excited to have her here. Used to solitude, he'd assumed he would loath someone else invading his private space.

But with her, it felt different. He wasn't losing anything. Instead, he felt like he was gaining much more than he deserved.

He'd had enough time to reflect on his past life. Both the good days and the sorrowful days. The gloomy days when they had lost young soldiers to the Al-Shabaab militants. The good days when he could loosen his guard and know that no harm would come his way or his colleagues. He felt like a blind man groping in the dark without the army.

When he heard her shower running, he knew he liked her company more than the quiet times alone. He was tired of living in the past and beating himself up for the past errors. He wanted to stay in the present, live in it and savour every flavour it was bringing his way. When life gave you an egg, you made an omelette.

As he passed by her door, he was tempted to tell her goodnight. But he knew that was just an excuse because what he wanted to do was join her in the shower. Was her skin as smooth as he imagined? He increased his pace and headed for his room. He had to control himself or else...

She was too vulnerable to indulge in the pleasures his flesh was craving.

***

The following day, Akinyi ran her errands.

First, she went to see her mother and then to the office. She had a lot of reports to write and stayed in the office until five o'clock in the evening.

She checked on her mother, ensuring she was sound asleep before heading to Adams' home. It felt strange going there. She walked at a slow pace feeling the breeze on her face.

When she arrived, it was already dark. She found Adams seated on the porch with a faraway look and a cigarette between his fingers.

"Hey," she whispered, startling him.

"Hey. I didn't hear you come," he said quickly, putting off the cigarette and motioning for her to sit next to him.

The air was still filled with the smell of cigarettes. She didn't like the odour. She was tempted to ask him why he smoked but didn't get to it. It was his house, and he could do as he pleased. It was none of her business as long as he didn't smoke when she was around.

The cricket chirped, and dark clouds hung in the sky. The wind blew violently. When it started to drizzle, they went into the house.

"It's too early to eat supper. Can we sit in the living room for a while?" Adams asked.

"That's fine by me. Let me take a bath first."

"Go ahead," Adams said, his face lighting up. The dark mood that she had found him in was now gone.

Akinyi rose and went to her bedroom. She showered and applied lotion to her body, massaging her shoulders to remove the knots there. She was at a loss for what to wear. She could not put on her nightdress. It was very transparent, and she didn't want to put ideas into his head. She chose an orange dress that went slightly beyond the knees. It was more decent.

She came out after twenty minutes and sat beside him on the couch. He had already put on some music, and soda was on the table. He poured some into a glass and handed it to her. The refined beats of the music filled the room.

***

"How was work today?" Adams asked. Swallowing hard, he shifted in his seat. The chocolate smell of Akinyi's lotion was making him unsettled. The orange dress did wonderful things to her voluptuous figure.

"It was full of report writing," she answered, oblivious to his turmoil.

They sipped their drinks in silence.

Adams wondered how long he was going to control himself with her here. He had never shared his house with a woman before without having sex, and it was playing havoc with his feelings. He had always gone to his mistress with the main idea of getting laid. He had gotten wired that having a woman meant lots of lovemaking. He watched her gulping her drink uncomfortably and wondered if she was having similar thoughts

"Are you ready to eat now?" he asked, and when she nodded, they went to the dining room.

The aroma of deliciously fried fish wafted in the air. They ate the meal while watching the news. Afterwards, she cleared the plates, took them to the sink and declared that she would go to bed early.

Adams listened to more music after she left. His body was taut with built-up desires.

He needed a woman—one woman, to be precise.

The urge to walk to her door and knock made his skin itch. Instead, he drained the beer and walked to his room.

***

Once she locked the door, she leaned on it, trying to breathe normally. Was she wrong in agreeing to her mother's plea? This was proving more difficult than she thought. While she was sitting next to Adams, she craved the taste of his mouth. She knew first-hand how the feeling made her come alive. Was it wrong to crave the pleasures of the flesh?

She knew he had been thinking of it, too, from how he kept eyeing her when he thought she was not looking. She almost opened the door and walked back to him in the sitting room.

No. Shaking her head, she walked to her bed and sat on the edge. With one final glance at the door, she eased back the covers and got into bed.

CHAPTER NINETEEN

They spent the next few days in awkward silence, each keeping their thoughts to themselves. However, one evening Adams invited Akinyi to the porch. They had a long conversation and the initial unease melted.

Now Akinyi looked forward to their nights on the porch when they could talk easily without any pressure or expectations.

Tonight as they listened to the chirping crickets, she decided to ask him about life in the army.

"I knew I wanted to be a soldier when I was young. I saw the Rambo and Jackie Chan movies, and I fell in love instantly. I even moulded soldiers and guns with clay," he said, looking so nostalgic.

Akinyi tried to picture him as a child. Had he been one of the tall boys in the village? She wanted to ask but didn't want to interrupt the story.

"When I finished high school, there was recruitment in the neighbouring school, so I went to try my luck. My father gave some kitu kidogo, and I was among the successful recruits," he continued.

"Were you happy or scared?" she asked, sipping her drink.

He paused for a while before saying, "I was ecstatic. It was like a dream come true. I was going to fight to defend my beloved country. I had only believed in the romantic version of being a soldier. I didn't know that I was signing up to be a gun for hire."

Akinyi almost kicked herself hard for probing into his life, but she wanted to understand. She had always believed that ignorance was bliss, but she would no longer be kept in the dark. If she was going to share some time with this man, she had to know him more deeply and dive below the surface.

"That sounds disappointing for a young man who had spent his waking hours and sleeping time dreaming of being a soldier," she commented, and he nodded in agreement.

"The training had been hell. Training hard for long hours, little sleep, the insults, and the whipping. They had told us that they were converting us from civilians to soldiers. In a real sense, they amputated our soft spots and turned us into monsters. We were only comfortable and could drop our guards around fellow soldiers. A soldier must be tough. They call it being army strong. We were told that our role was to take lives. Therefore, we needed psychological training on ruthlessness," he said, his eyes clouding with something dark.

She could not fathom the emotions they were conveying. She had thought that she could understand his work, but she had been wrong. There was no way of understanding it by watching from outside the fence. One had to live the life, walk in his shoes to begin to understand.

He cleared his voice and continued, "The real test was when we went for the Linda Nchi operation. They told us that we would defend our country but who was defending us. They always said that—mungu ni wa majeshi—we were left in the hands of God."

She couldn't help it. She took his hands into hers when she saw the tormented look in his eyes. His hands were freezing cold. For a moment, she thought that he would pull his hands away, but when he didn't, she warmed them with hers.

"Did you lose any of your friends?" she asked when she saw that he had relaxed and his hands were gaining heat.

"A lot of my friends paid the ultimate price. Al-Shabaab militants ambushed us several times, and we kept losing soldiers. One night, three of my closest friends were killed. I was mad at God, the Al-Shabaab and the government. I was almost running out of my mind. That night we went seeking them and killed a large number of them. But the pain even worsened. At the end of the day, we were all killers regardless of which interests we were serving. By killing them, were we better off? They were turning us into monsters, slowly but surely."

"Did your men ever rape any women?" she asked and regretted asking the question immediately when he jerked back, narrowing his eyes.

"War is cruel. That's all I can say. Unfortunately, some people use rape as a weapon of war. I don't condone it, but it's a reality. Now you have a glimpse into the life of a soldier."

"It is very informative," she said, straightening her tense shoulders.

The mood had shifted, and she had probed enough. She didn't have the stomach for further gory details of war. She had so many unanswered questions but tonight wasn't the night for them. They had more nights to talk for the foreseeable future.

***

One day in September, they sat on the porch as had become their routine.

"What is it like to be an only child?" Adams asked.

Akinyi smiled before saying, "It had both the good and the bad side. Which one do I start with?"

"The good."

" First, you get all the attention from your parents. Then, you are bought most toys."

"Only those?" he asked, raising one of his eyebrows.

"Pretty much. On the bad side, you are a solitary bird, flying solo. You have no siblings to play with, and you do all the household chores yourself. It gets lonely."

He considered what she had said, "Does that mean that you are always alone?"

"Yes, but the truth is I like my own company. My friend, Ephy, can't stand to be alone for long.

She gets depressed by the silence. What about you?"

"We are three in my family—my older brother, Seth, me and my younger sister, Val."

"Then it must have been fun growing up?"

"It was. We could play football with Seth the entire day. Val was born when I was in class six. By then, we didn't play much because of schoolwork. But on weekends, we would babysit while our mother did work around the house."

"I am jealous. Now that you are grown, are you still close?"

Adams looked into the dark sky, dreading the question. He could lie and get it over with.

"Sorry. You don't have to answer if you don't want to. I understand," she said quickly.

He was tempted to take the bait but thought better of it. He had never shared what happened with any living soul. Yet as he stared at her attentive expression, he wanted to tell her the truth about his wounds.

"I haven't seen them for a while."

"How long?"

"Seventeen years."

"Seventeen years!" she gasped. Something was not right.

He narrated the story about how they blamed him for the death of his mother.

She reached for his hands and looked at him sympathetically. Adams resisted the urge to pull away from the hold and pace the room or light a cigarette. He didn't deserve pity. Instead, he should be reprimanded and told that it was his fault.

"I am so sorry. How have you coped with being away that long?"

"I developed my own survival tactics. Sometimes I look back and wonder what I could have done right. Maybe if I hadn't joined the army, my mother would still be alive."

"You don't know that for sure. Nobody knows what the future holds."

He looked momentarily lost for words before saying, "I know, but that doesn't prevent me from wondering. When the pain gets too much, I light a cigarette and smoke the pain."

She smiled despite herself, feeling foolish for thinking it was just some bad habit. "I still think that Seth and your father accused you because grief clouded their better judgement."

"But I was also grieving. Imagine coming home to an already plastered grave. I felt so lost."

She squeezed his hand, and he shook his head, "Sorry for spoiling the evening. I have never told anyone about the incident."

She felt special and sad too. She could only imagine what he had lived through all the seventeen years. He was being brave about this, army strong.

"How come you have never told anyone about this? You have friends."

"In the army, one way of handling grief is to never talk about it. If you don't say anything about it, then time will dull the ache, and it will finally disappear. I guess I took that up."

She didn't know what to say to make this right. She stood from her seat and went to him, sitting on his lap and hugging him. Warm tears tracked down his cheek as he held her tightly. They stayed that way for long. When they later walked back into the house, it was apparent they had crossed an emotional boundary, and there was no going back.

CHAPTER TWENTY

Akinyi had mixed feelings. Sadness and emptiness from losing David clouded her days sometimes, and she didn't know what would take away the pain.

Also, she felt angry and stupid for believing in happy endings. She wasn't Cinderella, but who didn't want the happily ever after in their lives?

Maybe her mother had been right when she claimed that such love was better left to the movies and novels. But she had assumed it. Had believed that the four-letter word—LOVE—was magical and eternal. Now she didn't even know what to think.

"What are you thinking about? Adams asked

"Nothing much."

"From the look on your face, I can tell that it's something fierce and nasty."

"Since when did you become a mind reader?"

"With you, I have to be,"

"I was just wondering about love."

"What about it?"

"Do you believe that it exists?"

"Of course, it does."

"You seem so sure."

"I am. You should have seen how my parents loved each other. You would have drawn the same conclusion. Do you believe in it?"

"I used to."

"You are talking in the past tense."

"I know. I don't believe in it anymore. It seems something complicated. Besides, you don't always end up with the person you love."

Adams nodded in agreement.

"Have you ever been in love?" she asked, not looking at him, focusing on the starry sky.

He smiled before saying, "I have."

"What was it like?"

He shifted in his seat, crossing and uncrossing his legs. "I am not comfortable discussing another woman in your presence."

"Go ahead. I am curious. Don't turn me down."

"On one condition?"

"Which is?"

"You tell me yours too."

"Deal."

He chuckled and said, "I once loved a lady. She was called Salome Atieno. We met right after I had joined the army. Mostly we talked on the phone, she would visit me at the Kahawa barracks once every month, and when I had authorised leave, I went to her. The distance and army life didn't make it easy, but we were coping."

Akinyi was very attentive, leaning forward.

"Then we went for the operation Linda Nchi in Somalia, and things nosedived. Getting a network was impossible unless we went to the nearest

145

shopping centre miles away. I rarely called her, and when she tried to call me, I was out of reach. I thought she understood that I was at work."

"But she did not?"

"No, when I was able to contact her, it was after months. She was mad at me. I was mad at her for being inconsiderate. The phone calls turned into screaming battles. I had the missions to think about already. I could not take it anymore. I began to dread the phone calls. Then I hated them. Even if I could get a network, I would not call her. I was being unfair to her."

"Did you manage to solve your issues?"

"I wish we had. But when I came home after eight months, she had moved in with a man."

"What?"

"Yes, I even bumped into them during my leave. They looked so happy and in love. I greeted them and walked away."

"How did that make you feel?"

"Jealous, mad. She should have waited for me. I was again reminded of my sad, lonely life. The war is cruel and knowing that nobody is waiting at home to receive you with open arms makes it even worse."

"I guess life is a bitch," she said, adjusting the leso that covered her legs.

"I met her six months ago in town. She had left the man. She wanted to make a comeback."

"Did you accept?"

He chuckled before saying, "After she left me twisting in the wind, no way. I forgave her, but I just could not take her back."

"Pride?"

"Yes, sometimes you have to be proud, have self-worth and whatnots."

"True."

"Now, it is your turn? Enlighten me about your love life."

"My love life is not that rosy. Plus, today was about you. I promise to tell you tomorrow."

"Why do I feel like I have been tricked?"

"No, I haven't tricked you. Tomorrow is D-Day."

"A promise is a debt," he said, standing up. She rose too, and they went into the house.

***

Akinyi arrived home feeling depressed. She dragged her feet and sat heavily on the steps, staring into the twilight.

She'd just visited her mother, whose condition had worsened, signalling the end. The pain in the older woman's eyes made her wish to end the suffering, which unfortunately meant death as there was no cure.

Adams had gone to repair the fence, and he returned to find her on the steps.

"What's wrong?"

"Nothing, I am just tired."

He walked into the house and came out with icy water. She drank a glassful and felt good.

"How is my mother-in-law?"

"Not good. She is wasting away," she said in a whisper.

"Maybe, we should take her to the hospital."

"But she said that she didn't want to die in some cold hospital bed surrounded by strangers."

"I want to see her. We can convince her to go to the hospital. Let me change my clothes, and then we can leave," he said and went into the house.

He came back after five minutes, and they left. They found some relatives in the sitting room. Akinyi's mother was resting on the bed. She was snoring and groaning. Adams held Akinyi's hand, and they sat on the stools next to the bed.

"Mama," Akinyi called, wiping her sweat with a handkerchief.

Her mother stirred awake and whispered, "Water." Akinyi left the room to fetch the water. Adams held her bony hand and looked into her hollow, almost lifeless eyes. Her breathing was rugged, and tears began rolling down her face.

"Take...care...of...her...please," she said and began stretching out, struggling and her eyes staring blankly.

Adams held onto her hand as she exhaled her last breath. Warm tears rolled down his face. Was God giving him a second chance to see and clutch his mother's hand as she passed on?

He heard the falling and shattering of the glass and turned. Akinyi stood behind him. Her face was pallid, eyes wide open, and mouth agape. He rushed to her and gathered her into his arms. It took a while for her to begin sobbing. The relatives rushed in, and Adams led her out of the room.

***

Akinyi could not even recall the day's activities. She had been in a daze, drifting in and out.

Adams took the body to the morgue, and funeral arrangements began.

After the burial, Adams looked for Akinyi everywhere but could not find her. He was becoming worried. Where had she gone to? Was she alright? She had become distant and silent after her mother died.

His heart ached for her, wishing he could take her grief away. He missed his old Sexy Back. He missed her smile, her loud laughter that usually echoed through the house. He missed bantering with her. He had taken all those things for granted. Now, he understood that you never miss the water until the well runs dry.

He walked into her room in total darkness and heard sobbing. He was about to switch on the lights but changed his mind. His eyes got accustomed to the dark, and he saw her on the floor on her knees and her head cast down, sobbing. Something sharp pierced through his heart. He went to her and sat on the floor beside her. She turned to look at him, and he took her into his arms.

"Hush now, baby. Hush," he soothed her, rubbing her back with one hand and her face with the other.

Akinyi snuggled closer to his body, holding him tightly and more tears flowed down her face. Each time she stopped, she would remember that she was all alone in the world and start all over.

When the cry subsided, she asked, "Why does life sometimes have to be so unfair. I am all alone, Adams. I don't have any siblings. My father is gone, and now my mother and ...."

He released her. "But, Sexy Back, you have your grandma and me. I am here for as long as you need me. I'm not going anywhere. I promise."

She looked into his eyes and saw something she hadn't noticed before. Something she couldn't put the finger on. But whatever it was, it made her heart beat faster.

"I wish I could just throw caution to the wind and glide in the waves," she said, finally playing with one of his buttons.

"But what is stopping you, baby? You can take a chance on me."

"It is easier said than done. I once gave my heart, and it got bruised so badly. But, with your loving care, I am finding myself caring for you, but I am afraid."

"Don't be. What was the name of that stupid bastard?"

Akinyi slightly smiled through her tears. "David Ouko, sir."

"This David needs some thorough beating. Where can I find him?" His lips formed a straight line, and she knew he was serious.

She had imagined several ways in which David could be punished.

"I don't know where he is. Since we broke up last November, I haven't talked to him, and I don't think I want to." She had a pained look on her face.

Adams knew she was lying, but he didn't point it out. Some minutes passed before he spoke, "He must have meant the world to you."

She nodded to confirm his words. He felt jealous even though he didn't even know David.

He felt jealous because the David guy was still engraved in her heart after all this time. He hadn't found a woman who cared for him the same way. He had seen how his parents were so much in love and had envied them.

Yet, somehow, he hadn't managed to command such love from a woman. He didn't know why. Still, the army life wasn't conducive to relationships, which needed spending so much time together. And as fate would have it, that had been a luxury he could not afford.

Lost in his thoughts, he didn't realise she'd fallen asleep until he noticed her eyes closed and breathing regular. He was holding her in his arms, but something was still missing. He felt so empty deep within, lonely. Maybe even lonelier than her.

He wanted her to love him. Maybe even needed it, and these feelings were strange to him. He traced her face with his hands, touching her hair, eyelids, and nose.

Then he couldn't help lowering his lips and brushing her soft ones. It felt so good, so whole.

She shifted in his arms, and he pulled back quickly like a young boy who'd been caught stealing sugar.

Her eyes flew open, and he stared back innocently.

"Were you kissing me?" she asked, a naughty smile playing on her lips.

"I thought you were sleeping."

"Then now I am awake," she said, pulling him down to her and possessing his mouth. He kissed her thoroughly before pulling back. He didn't want to push beyond his threshold. He was just a man, made of flesh and bones.

"Let me put you to bed. It's getting cold," he said, carrying her to bed.

She frowned as if wondering what was wrong with him and why the change of mood.

She was still in her black dress and didn't seem to have the strength to change into her nightdress. He wanted to let her sleep in them to avoid tormenting himself, but one look at her tight dress, and he knew he had no option.

He cursed under his breath as he reached for the zip of her dress.

"Sit up, please, so we can remove your dress," he said hoarsely, not believing his voice.

She sat up, still sleepy. He slipped her dress off her and looked into her round wide-open eyes. He didn't trust himself to look at her body without touching it.

"You look like you have seen a ghost, Adams," she said lazily.

"Maybe I have," he said, slipping her nightdress through her head. When he finished without looking at her body, he promised himself a glass of beer for a job well done. He pulled the covers over her and turned to leave.

"Goodnight, baby. Dream of me." He went out of the door a tormented man, his body aching for her so much, so badly. He had been on a dry spell for so long it was finally catching up with him. He needed a cold shower.

CHAPTER TWENTY-ONE

Akinyi soaked her pillows as she curled up in her bed, her heart heavy with sadness. Loneliness gnawed away at her. Mama was no more and would never walk the earth again or hear her voice. All she had now were memories of her.

Adams was trying to be there for her in her hour of need, but what were his true feelings? Their agreement was to last until after the burial. She couldn't believe that she would abandon this lovenest they had made for themselves, but their marriage was based on a lie. A beautiful lie.

She quickly got up, bathed, and packed her small bag lest he came back and found her. It was already thirty minutes past seven.

She knew that it was proper to say goodbye. But goodbye was such a bitch. Her speciality was in saying hello. She quickly scribbled a note for him on a paper and left it in the middle of the bed where she was sure he wouldn't miss it.

She stood up and looked at the room as a tear escaped her eyes. Her life was flipped on its head, and nothing was familiar anymore. How would she ever survive without Adams' bedroom eyes, tempting lips and smooth caresses that held beautiful promises? She had to endure one way or the other. She turned and walked out of the room, closing the door, hushing the memories.

On her way out, she met Mama Awino in the corridor.

"Why are you crying? And where are you going to at this hour?" the woman asked, looking Akinyi up and down, her face marred with worry.

"I am leaving. Please tell Adams not to worry about me," she whispered, more tears threatening to flow.

"What do you mean you are leaving? For good?" she asked, her face becoming pale.

Akinyi nodded.

"Don't do this! It will kill him," she pleaded.

"I'm dying inside too. It wasn't an easy choice. I have to go, please. Bye." Akinyi moved past her and out into the night.

A boda-boda motorist was already waiting for her by the gate. She climbed on it, and it sped away, the breeze cooling her fevered face. Within fifteen minutes, she was in Oyugis town. She booked the Transline bus to leave in the next thirty minutes.

She quickly ate supper in one of the hotels and bought water supplies, snacks and chewing gum. By the time she was through, the bus was about to leave. She didn't know for how long she would stay away from the town. She would return when her life was in perspective. She had to come back.

***

Adams parked his car in the garage and walked into the house, whistling. He had gone to Kisumu to meet up with potential clients.

"Why haven't you gone home, Mama Awino?" he asked when he found her seated in the dining room dozing off.

She stood up with a start. "I wanted to give you the keys."

He hesitated, looking about the room, searching for Akinyi. "Why would you want to give me the keys? Where is Akinyi?"

"She left one hour ago." Rubbing her hands together, avoiding his gaze.

He raised his eyebrows and asked, "Where did she go?"

"She did not tell me. You need to find her," she said urgently, handing him the keys and walking out.

He took them, the news settling on his stomach with a thud. How could she just up and leave? Why didn't she wait for him?

He walked to her room and saw that most of her belongings were still there. He took out his phone and tried to reach her, but she wasn't picking up his calls. Hopefully, she hadn't already left the town.

He climbed into his car, his heart thudding and sped to town, hoping and praying that she hadn't already left.

When he got to Oyugis, he searched in vain at all the bus stations. Had her bus left town already? He tried her number again, but the call went to voicemail. He rubbed his face frantically, at a loss. He went back to his car to calm himself down, counting one to ten. Then, rubbing his stiff neck, he accepted her decision. She must have a good reason for leaving.

He drove back to the house dejectedly. The love song playing in the background irked him, and he switched off the radio, opening the windows. The night air was cool against his skin.

When he finally packed his car, even climbing the stairs to the house took much effort. He walked to her room and sat on the bed.

She was truly gone. Was it true that the one who was left often felt more grief than the one who left? Her pink nightie lay on the bed, mocking him. He reached for it, fisted and pressed it to his nose, closing his eye. Why did she have to leave? He kept asking himself, but no answer could suffice.

He saw the note on the bed. Trepidation hummed in his fingers as he read it.

Dear Adams,
I never wanted to leave the way I did. But I had no choice. I am not good at saying goodbyes. I hope you understand.
Akinyi

She had no choice? Anger flared inside him.

She could have stayed with him, but she chose to walk away. How was he supposed to understand her leaving when she gave him no reason?

He felt like smashing something hard against the wall but reached for his cigarettes and lighter. Sitting outside, he smoked, wondering where Akinyi was. He missed her with a hunger deep in his guts.

***

Akinyi went to stay with her friend, Ephy, in Kahawa. The next day they were doing window shopping in Nairobi town. Ephy wanted to buy a handbag for the upcoming date with some hot-looking ambassador.

"Please, let's find this magic bag faster. My legs are killing me," Akinyi complained.

"Don't even start. You think I've forgotten how you made us walk when you were looking for David's valentine present," Ephy countered, and they looked at each other and broke into a laugh.

"And speaking of magic, is that David?" Ephy asked, rubbing her eyes to get a clearer view.

Akinyi slapped her on the arm. "Don't joke about the impossibilities."

"I wish I was joking. Look," she said, pointing.

Her serious expression nudged Akinyi to look over her shoulder.

Her heart skipped a beat when she saw David, the height, the walk, and the army haircut.

This could not be true. David was supposed to be in Mombasa, but maybe he was on leave. She was still looking at him when suddenly he turned in her direction.

She had told Ephy that if she happened to bump into him one day, she would run away. But she didn't even have the strength in her legs.

Recognition dawned on David when he saw her and the surprised look on his face told it all. They stared at each other, the memories rushing back just in one glance. Time stood still. The passers-by were unnoticed. The hooting of the cars and the hawkers' noises could not penetrate this surreal moment.

Akinyi remembered the kisses, the caresses, the plans of being Mrs Ouko, the breakup, the disappointment, the bitterness. And she hated the very sight of him. How could he have hurt her so much when he had claimed to love her? Had it all been a bluff? Or was she just another case of love casualty?

She turned in the opposite direction and walked on, tears blurring her vision. She almost ran over one of the beggars on the pavements, and he yelled insults at her.

Ephy followed, half running behind her on the street. "Stop!"

Akinyi stopped suddenly and turned to her. Ephy hugged her, telling her that all was going to be okay. Akinyi wished she could believe her, believe in something, like a drowning man clutching at a straw.

By the time they pulled apart, David was by their side. Akinyi wanted to walk away, but there was something in his eyes, pleading.

"How are you?" he asked in that smooth voice that Akinyi had come to love, and she almost threw her hands up in frustration.

She didn't answer, but it didn't matter because Ephy chipped in too cheerfully, announcing that they were fantastic.

"I'm sorry, Akinyi. I didn't mean for things to end the way they did," he said too quickly, like this was something he wanted to put behind them and even pretend that it hadn't occurred.

Not happening. Akinyi refused to let him off the hook easily. He had broken her heart, taken her for a ride and tossed her aside like yesterday's rubbish.

"I already forgave you. It's not that you deserve it, but I never want my heart to turn into a heart of stone and ice. You aren't capable of loving anyone else," Akinyi said, wiping her tears away with the back of her hand.

"Mum, don't cry," he said, wiping her tears with his thumb.

Akinyi moved away, hissing, "Don't you dare touch me."

A lady appeared beside David and had been with him the first time Akinyi had seen him on the street. But it hadn't clicked that they might be together. She had a tiny baby in her arms.

"And who is this?" Akinyi asked, looking from David to the woman.

The lady was short and wore a cheap mitumba dress that didn't quite suit her figure. She appeared average-looking, just another face in the crowd.

"I am Mrs Ouko. What are you saying to my husband?" she asked, looking at Akinyi in disgusted,

Akinyi barely noticed, still absorbing what the lady had uttered. She sneered at David. So much for wanting to work things out! Instead, she hated him passionately, wiping out the love she had once felt for him.

Turning, she walked away, knowing this time it was for good.

David had been married with a child all this time. Yet they had broken up less than a year ago.

The only explanation was that he had been dating the other lady while they were still an item. She wished that she had not known. She could have just gone through life wondering what could have gone wrong.

But then again, she would have wasted valuable time beating herself up. She didn't know how she was going to survive this. She had started to heal, but now it was like the wound had been freshly opened again.

She walked away, half running to get away from him as fast as possible.

CHAPTER TWENTY-TWO

Akinyi was quiet throughout the journey to Kahawa. Ephy tried to strike some conversation but only received nods and forced smiles. She had even vainly tried the funny videos she had downloaded from WhatsApp. Finally, she gave up and left Akinyi to her own mulling.

"Please say something, Akinyi," Ephy pleaded when they arrived home.

Akinyi just looked at her from across the room and threw her hand up in resignation. Her eyes filled with unshed tears.

"Don't worry about me. I'll be fine in the morning. I just want to lie down for a while."

"You still love him, don't you?" Ephy asked as if daring her to deny it.

"I don't," she said, too loudly, too quickly.

"You lying bitch! Go on convincing yourself otherwise, but we both know that you still do."

"Are you forcing me to feel what I don't," she countered, smiling at Ephy's effort.

"Not that you need any encouragement, but if that was your replacement that I saw, you should be laughing your heart out instead of sitting here and playing the victim,"

"She was beautiful," Akinyi mumbled.

"In an ugly kind of way. How could he replace you with such a low life? He has no shame. You deserve better."

"You are just saying that to cheer me up."

"Yes, but it is also the truth."

"You know, at the back of my mind, I harboured this stupid idea of us getting back together, a foolish idea. I thought it was like the previous misunderstandings and that we would work things and remain an item."

"I can give you that. You never imagined it could end. I have to admit that I am also surprised. You were always the ideal couple. It was headed for the happily ever after,"

"Yeah, funny how life turns out. I always thought that immediately after campus, we were going to move in together and start our lives, have a couple of children, and grow old together," Akinyi said.

They broke into hysterical laughter that brought tears to their eyes.

"Ephy, you are the best. Thanks for being here with me. I don't know what I could have done without you. I now know why some people commit suicide."

"You would have done simply fine, trust me."

"That reminds me, the last time we saw each other, David asked me whether I would commit suicide if he chose to walk out on me."

"There are always signs before they leave, like a headlight, warning you of the impending danger. It's just that sometimes we choose to ignore it or are too scared to accept the signs for what they are."

"Very true."

"Like when he refused to see me while on leave. He always said that he was busy. I found it creepy, but I gave him many chances to make it right by me. He just blew all of them."

"Let's go out and drink our sorrows away," Ephy suggested, getting off the couch.

"That's always your solution to all problems. Don't you know that we are no longer on campus and should behave responsibly if we want to get married? My mother always maintained that there was no way you could find a decent man in a club."

"We are not going to look for husbands, plus it's pretty late to go to church," Ephy said, winking.

"Ephy, you never change."

"I haven't found any reason to. Why should we wallow in our sorrow when we can go out and make merry? The bill is on me. Get going, you lazy bone."

Akinyi found the idea of going out too enticing to brush off. She hit the shower in five minutes. After fifteen minutes, they were applying foundation on their faces, mascara for their eyes and red lipstick that her mother had complained always made one look like they had dipped their mouths in blood.

Akinyi was in a glittery black dress while Ephy wore a noticeably short blue outfit which accentuated her thin waist and large butt. They took their handbags and left the house.

They took a bus to town with blaring music, which was just what they needed to get into the clubbing mood. Life was too short to spend it lamenting what life had taken from you.

When they got to Mojos' Club, it was packed to capacity, yet it was only a little past nine. They found their seats by the balcony. Ephy ordered a bottle of Amarula and the waitress brought them some ice to go with it.

Mejja's 'Get Down' hit was playing, reminding them of carefree campus days. So they got up and danced with some guys.

By the time the next song came on, they were already sweating. So they returned to their seats to resume their drinking.

"These people don't know how to have fun. Look at them just sitting down," Akinyi shouted to be heard over the loud music.

"They are old and tired. The working-class men and women listen more to the music than doing 'Bendova'," Ephy said, sipping her wine.

"Ooh, I'm not that old yet, and besides, I don't have the belly which I can babysit on the couch while dancing to the music with my head and hands. Let's go home."

"I hope that by home, you mean Scratch,"

"Of course, where else? Let's go to our sufferers. They are livelier and vibrant. All I want to do is shake my body all night long."

"Don't kill me with laughter. Our 'sufferers' are livelier because they only have five hundred shillings to spare from their loan for drinking. So they avoid drinking all their money by dancing three-quarters of the time while taking small sips of their cheap liquor," Ephy said.

They used to do the same. It seemed like ages ago, yet it wasn't so long ago.

"OK, Madam. Let's finish this baby here and leave," Akinyi said, motioning to the half-empty bottle.

My Name Is Roberto, Amarula came from the speakers, and most of the people in the club got up and showed their best-kept skills on the dance floor.

Ephy lifted their bottle high, shouting, "Amarula."

They left one hour later, staggering to the Scratch Club. The cool Nairobi night air did some work in sobering them.

"We are the modern women described by Kingang'i in classic radio. Beer-guzzling, nyama choma and mutura-eating women who spend their nights in clubs," Ephy slurred her words, and they laughed.

"This is a whole new world, and I feel brand new," Akinyi announced, and Ephy ululated into the night.

After being screened at the entrance, they climbed the stairs leading to the club slowly like their legs had turned to jelly. By the time they got to the club, they were panting.

They paid their entrance fees and went in. The air was already charged with sweat, and it was stuffy. Nevertheless, almost everyone was up on their feet, dancing the night away. They squeezed their way through the crowd, trying to find a dancing space.

Weka Weka was the name of the song. The campus dudes were shouting, jumping, and dancing like their lives depended on it. By the time the music slowed down to Techno, they were tired. They headed for the washrooms.

"I guess we are getting old. The vigorous dancing is becoming too much for me," Akinyi commented.

"Maybe it's because you spend too much time in the shagz. You should go out more," Ephy told her as they queued in the ladies.

"Easier said than done. If I do that in the shagz, the elders will certainly curse me. The only reasonable club in Oyugis is Blazer Club, where most men in the town hang out on weekends."

"And there are high chances of running into them. Imagine meeting your uncles, grandfather, or cousins in the club."

"It will be the town gossip for a long time. Flaws of living in a small town where everyone knows everyone,"

"Exactly my point. You should come to Nairobi so that we hustle for the good life."

"But still, I love the small town with my whole heart. You know I am not a city girl like you."

"I know."

They went back to the club and resumed their seats. They ordered Del Monte because they didn't want to chew blackout.

"Look at that man over there," Ephy exclaimed, looking at her target.

"You are crazy, I swear. You said that you were not looking for a husband in the club."

"Who said it has to lead to marriage. You take life too seriously. I'm just feasting my eyes, nakula kwa macho."

"While keeping the gun in the store. You are team Mafisilet, I swear."

The man caught Ephy staring, but she didn't even blink. The man looked away after sometimes.

"Ephy, the man is coming," Akinyi said.

The man strode to their table, and she knew immediately that he was Ephy's type. He was beautiful, a little chubby and brown.

"Ladies, how is the night so far?" the man asked, smiling and looking at Ephy.

Akinyi didn't see the need to answer because she was clearly out of the equation. Instead, she sipped her drink while her ears listened to the conversation.

"OK, Ephy, it was nice knowing you. I will give you a call," the man said, shaking her hand.

Ephy said softly, "And I will answer."

Akinyi stifled a laugh after the man left.

"What are you laughing at?" her friend asked, sliding her phone back into her handbag.

"You just go for what you want. My go-getter friend."

"I have to. I can't wait around for things to be handed to me. I have to work my butt off."

Akinyi laughed and knew that with Ephy around, there was no way one could get bored.

By the time they were ready to leave, it was 4 o'clock. They walked out of the club, giggling and laughing from the effect of alcohol. They hailed a taxi and hopped into it.

"You remember how we used to board the Matatu feeling sleepy and then having to walk the one kilometre to Ngong hostel. It was pure punishment."

"Yeah, how can I forget? We would always wish somebody would use abracadabra on us after the night so we would just find ourselves wrapped warmly between our blankets."

CHAPTER TWENTY-THREE

Akinyi and Ephy alighted from the taxi, staggering and laughing for no reason. As they approached the house, Akinyo saw a figure hunched at the doorstep.

"Who is this drunkard at my door?" Ephy asked

"Look at the pot calling the cattle black. You think if you are drunk, everyone is," Akinyi said, laughing too loudly.

"Or it is that boy who has been stalking me since last week. Let's find out."

Akinyi abruptly turned to Ephy and said, "Slap me hard across the face."

"Why would I do that?" Ephy asked, rubbing her hands together in preparation for the slap.

"Because I think I have just seen a ghost."

A loud slap jolted her, and she rubbed her stinging cheek. "What was that for?"

"I thought you asked me to slap you?"

"Yes, but that was a figurative speech."

"Sorry."

"It's alright. Our drunkard is David."

"No way," Ephy exclaimed, rushing to the door to confirm. A closer look revealed a dozing, and cold David slumped on the doorstep. He still had the same clothes they had seen him in earlier that day.

Akinyi slapped him on the cheek as if repaying Ephy's slap on her. David stirred with a start, still confused, and it took him thirty seconds to find his bearing.

"What do you want?" she asked impatiently.

"I want many things," David said, lowering his voice to a whisper.

Suddenly Akinyi remembered the day they had made out in the ocean. It had started in the same fashion. A shiver ran down her spine at the memory, which was so distant yet so near.

The wicked light in his eyes indicated he knew what he was doing and liked the results.

"Get in the house before you freeze to death," Ephy called out, and they followed her inside.

Akinyi wished she could slam the door on his face to wipe out the stupid smugness on his face. But, since it wasn't her house, her hands were tied. She slumped on the couch with a thud, wondering where the drowsiness had gone.

David sat beside her after a while.

"Shouldn't you be home giving warmth to your wife and child?" Akinyi asked.

David chuckled before saying, "They can do without me tonight."

Ephy took water from the fridge and hurried to her room like she couldn't get away fast enough.

Akinyi wondered whether she was rushing off to sleep or to give them a chance to talk, or both.

They were left alone in the sitting room, staring at each other. Akinyi knew that ex-lovers were like a disaster waiting to happen. Give them some privacy, and the next thing would be an explosion because ex-lovers need no introduction. They were always familiar with each other's territory, knew what to expect and the right buttons to push to achieve the desired results.

Akinyi cleared her voice as the silence stretched. "I'm very sleepy. Talk fast."

"I wanted to explain why I left the way I did."

"Does it really matter right now?"

"Yes, it does."

"I don't think so. How could you just walk away without looking back?"

"It was a tough decision. It was you that I wanted to marry."

"Ooh!" she feigned surprise.

"Don't be so sarcastic. I know I did you wrong by sleeping with another woman but getting her pregnant is unforgivable."

"Is there a difference? A betrayal is a betrayal, David. I wonder why you have to keep me up at this ungodly hour trying to justify your behaviour."

"I'm sorry, Akinyi, I wish I could turn back the hands of time."

"How did you meet?" Akinyi asked the question that had been bugging her.

"We were just friends."

"Looking for benefit?"

"Pardon?"

"Were you friends looking for benefit?" Akinyi expounded.

171

"No, just friends. Trust me."

Speaking of trust, he didn't know how much she distrusted him. He had no right to use that word in her presence.

"One day, during one of her visits, we watched some movies, and it started raining. She could not go back to her house and had to spend the night at my place. One thing led to another. You know how these things go,"

"No, I don't. I know that while I was beating myself up for being the cause of our breakup while the fault was all yours."

"All mine? Give me a break. After your father died, you became distant."

"Are you apportioning blame? I was mourning my father."

"And I was missing you. I wanted to be with you, talk to you on the phone."

"Are you trying to justify your behaviour?"

"No. The point is that I was lonely, and she was always there for me."

"Oh."

"Say something, please."

"What is there to say? My father died, and while I mourned him for two months, you got another woman pregnant and married her."

"I am sorry. I should have been there for you."

"You should have, but you were not. But who are we kidding? You started pulling away long before the death of my father."

"That's not true," he said earnestly.

"It is. You started calling less frequently."

"My friends always told me that a graduate wife was going to be tough-headed, rude and leave me when she finds a fellow graduate." He shifted in his seat.

"Your friends? I thought you knew me better than that."

"I thought that I did. When you visited me and always complained about the housework? Sometimes you even refused to go when I sent you on errands. My worst fears were confirmed."

"So, what has changed now? I am still a graduate, and housework is still not my cup of tea."

"Honestly, I don't know why I am here. I know that I'm married and have a child. My wife is very submissive and a form-four leaver. She treats me like a king, yet...."

"Yet?"

"I still miss you. I miss your fire. I miss you pushing me to achieve greater and finer things."

"That's good to know, but you realize that it's too late for us. You are married. I am married too."

"What?" He appeared completely surprised. Beads of sweat formed on his forehead. He stood and paced the room.

Akinyi's mouth pouted into a smile.

"When did you get married?" he asked after taking his seat.

"Three months ago. I could not wait forever."

"I know. Do you love him?"

She considered the question. What was love?

"If love means what I once felt for you; the madness, craziness and stupidity, then the answer is no."

"What is that supposed to mean?"

"I have grown up. I am no longer that naïve girl you fell in love with six years ago. I look for different things in men these days. Love can grow, as my mother used to say. May God rest her soul in peace."

His face creased into a frown, "Your mother died too? Why didn't you tell me? I could have come to the funeral."

"For what?"

"How do you feel?" he asked, ignoring her sarcasm.

Feel? What did it mean to feel? Was it the ability to express sadness or happiness? For a long time, she had been numb.

"I feel fine, sad but fine. I know each person walks with some pain in their hearts."

The last thing she wanted from David was pity. Because he was then going to hug her to comfort her. She wasn't sure she could get close to him without getting scalded. She knew how comfort usually transforms into risky pleasures.

"I am so sorry," he said, pulling her in for a hug despite her reluctance.

When he held her close to his heart and wrapped his arm around her, tears escaped her eyes. She had once felt safe in his arms, but now it was just a bittersweet reminder of what she had lost. She hated herself for breaking down in front of him.

"Please, I beg you, forgive me. I know I can't undo the past and make things right," he whispered.

She pulled back from him. This was not a clever idea.

"You are right. You can't. Please, can I now go to bed?" she asked, wiping tears with the back of her hand.

"Have you forgiven me?" he asked hopefully.

"I told you I had, but I will never forget to steer clear of men of your kind," she said, looking at him in disgust. She got up from her seat, and he got up too. She thought he was following her to the door, but he had other ideas up his sleeves.

He held her from behind and pulled her to him. For a moment, she was transported back to the old days with his scent and touch.

Then a sick feeling replaced the sensation, and she pushed him away. "Don't touch me."

"Why not?" he asked.

"You shouldn't be asking that question. I have a thousand and one reasons. I would appreciate it if you left now."

"Let's enjoy ourselves one last time, for old times' sake," he pleaded.

"That's what all this has been reduced to, an old times' sake affair. Get out!" she hissed, opening the door.

Sighing, he walked out, and she slammed the door.

***

Akinyi leaned on the door, still trying to grasp what had happened. It seemed like the reverse of some tragic love story. It didn't seem real that David had just been here. Were it not for his scent on her skin, she would have sworn it had been a

175

figment of her imagination. She bolted from the door and rushed to bed. She found Ephy fast asleep and thanked God because she wasn't in the mood to talk about it. And she knew how Ephy could have wrung her dry of all the juicy details.

As she slipped on her nightgown, her mind rushed to Adams. Just the right image she needed to travel down the guilt path. She felt like she had cheated on him, yet he wasn't even her real husband, and even their fake marriage hadn't been consummated.

Adams had been good to her through and through, more than David had been. Yet amid past and present intertwining, he had slipped her mind.

She was glad that she had the mind to stop it. She didn't like where her thoughts were headed, so she covered herself with the duvet and closed her eyes tight. Sleep took over her tired body, relieving her of her misery temporarily.

CHAPTER TWENTY-FOUR

"Get up, Akinyi!" Ephy shook her awake.

"What is it?" Akinyi asked impatiently, closing her eyes again.

"Somebody is here to see you,"

"I hope it's not David."

"No. It's your fake husband."

"You have got to be kidding me, right? I left him in the heart of Oyugis' town."

"As if he is welded to that part of the town."

Akinyi was still trying to figure out what Ephy was saying when Adams breezed into the room.

His tall frame filled the room, commanding eyes to look at him because he was the centre of attraction. He was sp handsome. Why was she still glued to the past when the present was so tempting?

"Are you in the habit of ogling men?" he asked, reaching her side.

"Not always, except when they look so edible, and I am hungry," she teased.

Adams smiled, taking the chair by the bed. "Why are you sleeping in the afternoon? Are you sick?"

Akinyi laughed at the dumb question.

"No. I have a powerful hangover, and I think I'm going to be sick." She rushed to the bathroom.

Feeling weak, she returned to the room, head throbbing and stomach churning. She sat on the bed, embarrassed, covering her face with her hands.

"Are you surprised that I am drunk? Disappointed?"

"No. I'm worried about you. People drink heavily for various reasons. Sometimes because of stress and when they are running away from something. What are you running away from?"

"You."

"I don't believe you. You need to eat and take painkillers." Adams said, looking at her nightdress for the first time. It was a see-through dress that revealed more than it covered.

"And now you are ogling me?" Akinyi noted and smiled when he looked embarrassed at being caught in the act.

"I couldn't help myself. Sorry."

"It's OK. It is not every day that you find a man looking at you until he loses himself," she said, laughing, and he couldn't help but laugh too.

"Alright, intelligent woman, let me see how the soup is coming up," he said, leaving the room. She took the time to bathe quickly. When she finished, the aroma of fried beef met her nose, and she started salivating.

She dressed fast and joined the others in the sitting room. Food was already on the table.

"So, this is the Ephy you could not stop talking about?" Adams asked after praying.

"What! Were you gossiping about me?" Ephy asked, narrowing her eyes at her.

"Don't worry, I told him only the good stuff. For instance, you go to church every Sunday and don't even have a drop of alcohol in your blood. In fact, you are as innocent and sinless as baby Jesus," she told her, and they all laughed.

"Well, then maybe I can forgive and forget." Ephy looked like she was stifling another bout of laughter threatening to erupt.

When the meal was over, they chatted before Ephy left, claiming that she needed to lie down.

"How did you find me?" Akinyi asked.

"I asked around."

"Adhiambo told you where to find me. That girl can't keep a secret."

"Don't hold it against her. I was very persuasive."

"So why are you here?" Akinyi asked, closing the gap between them on the couch.

"To take my wife home."

"Fake wife."

"As long as the word 'wife' still features there," he said, winking at her.

"But the agreement was to end it once my mother died," she protested.

"I know, but that doesn't explain your escape without saying goodbye."

"It was necessary for me to get away as soon as possible."

"To get away from me?"

"You are only part of it. I had other issues I wanted to get away from. Don't take it personally."

"Ooh," he exclaimed, but Akinyi didn't give any more information.

"I have a place in town. Would you mind moving in with me?" he said after a while.

"I don't know. Ephy will think I am putting you before her," she explained, and Adams shook his head in disbelief.

She and Ephy had made a pact to put each other first regardless of the men who came into their lives. The men had come and gone, but their friendship had grown deeper with the passing years. It wasn't a pact that Akinyi wanted to break easily.

"Do you mind if I explain it to her?"

"Try your luck," she said, and he left to talk with her friend.

Ephy didn't like the idea but was happy for her. She bade them goodbye as they climbed into the car.

***

"Let's go into the club," Adams said, draining his glass of wine.

Akinyi looked around her. People milled around them, heading into the club. All her attention had been on his handsome face. He was sitting in the dimly lit bar, so poised and confident. She felt a shiver down her spine, thinking that he had come to Nairobi to find her.

He put his hand on the small of her back as he led her up the stairs to the Scratch club. His hands felt so right on her, like they were meant for her. She was concentrating on his hand that when he finally picked her up, she almost screamed out of surprise.

"What are you doing, Adams?" she asked, wiggling out of his arms, but his grip wasn't relenting, and she gave up.

"Just enjoy the ride while it lasts, Sexy Back," he said, continuing with the climb.

Two young ladies passed them, looked at Akinyi enviously and smiled sweetly at Adams.

She didn't know whether to be blush with embarrassment or punch into the air merrily. She leaned closer and kissed him on the left cheek.

Adams smiled his secret smile. When they finally reached the entrance, he reluctantly lowered her onto her feet. They spent the night dancing and drinking.

Adams couldn't contain his grin when he saw how the young women were bending over the men.

"Bend over is the name of the game," Akinyi said, pointing at the couple next to them

"I don't understand how the men can endure this. It's too erotic."

Akinyi shrugged as she sipped her Guarana. He looked at her again in the dim light and couldn't help noticing how beautiful she was.

The air was stuffy and smoky, the place packed with moving bodies. The music was too loud, making conversation almost impossible. So they went to club Samba for Rhumba. It was spacious. People were in groups chatting as a few swayed to the music.

When Madilu's System Colonisation came, he led her to the dancefloor, and they danced close, body to body. His arms resting on the small of her back, her arms around his neck.

Akinyi couldn't help but notice that all the 'bendovas' in the world couldn't come close to this. There was a thrill in subtlety—the anticipation, the promise of things to come and the glimpse into the possibility.

They left the club at 3 o'clock in the morning.

***

"I want us to go somewhere, and I hope you will like it," Adams said mysteriously.

"Where are you taking me, sir?" she asked curiously.

"It's a secret. If I tell you, I'll have to kill you," he said, not giving anything away.

"Give me some hints so that I don't go flying blind."

"Stubborn woman. We are going to shop for swimming costumes and hiking clothes. Does that give you a head start?"

"It does. Are we leaving tomorrow?" she asked, and he nodded.

Akinyi couldn't help the excitement rippling through her. She loved going out, and David had never been the outgoing kind of man. He didn't mind staying in the house for days, and she had always been bored.

It was not that she didn't like spending time with him, but all they did was cook, eat, wash utensils, and make love. Done every once in a while could be gratifying. However, it became so dull, so predictable when it was routine.

"Then you'll better dress up because we are leaving in the next thirty minutes," he announced.

She quickly got off the bed and went to the bathroom to freshen up. Afterwards, she dressed in a sky-blue dress that accentuated her hips.

"You look lovely," he said, giving her the once-over, and she blushed.

"Let's go then." She took her red sling bag, and he followed.

They walked into different shops looking at the best costumes. When they finally saw a red lacy outfit, she was thrilled.

Adams had never seen such a sexy piece of cloth, and he knew that it would look even better on her. In turn, he was going to be even in more trouble.

He took her to a candlelight dinner in one of the luxurious hotels in town, and he loved how she had a massive appetite for food.

***

"Wake up, sleepyhead. I want us to start the journey early before the jam catches up with us," Adams said, shaking her awake.

Akinyi opened her eyes to the glaring light of the bulb and covered her head with the blanket.

"Let me sleep for five more minutes, then I promise to wake up."

"You are lying. You will end up saying five more minutes endlessly."

"Please, you know I am not a morning person. Let's leave at 10 o'clock. The jam will have cleared," she pleaded so softly that he agreed.

He knew he was being teased with the sweet voice, but he couldn't help it.

He took his shower leisurely, feeling the water stir his senses to life. He didn't remember any time when showering had felt so reviving. Reluctantly, he left the warmth of the water to dry himself.

Akinyi woke up at around 8 o'clock, stretching and yawning. She found him already dressed up and busy on his desk reading. He looked up at her and smiled before asking her about her night.

"I slept soundly like a little baby," she said and fled to the bathroom.

She had caught Adams staring at her like he was trying to focus on the conversation. Akinyi knew that he had some wayward thoughts about her. She didn't know whether to be pleased or mad. She didn't want to spend her life being angry, so she whistled and sang loudly in the bathroom.

Adams shook his head in disbelief. There was just no end to the wonders of this woman. She had been dressed in her green pyjamas that didn't even cling to her body, yet he'd been tempted. Maybe it was the very idea of her body covered. He imagined undressing her like unwrapping a sweet to taste the real thing.

He was getting a hard-on just thinking about it. Her loud singing and whistling weren't helping matters, announcing her presence. He resumed reading the morning newspaper to distract from his cravings.

When they finally left the house, it was a little past 9 o'clock. Thika highway was clear of jams.

Akinyi stared at his hands on the steering wheel, reminding her of their first meeting. When she glanced at him, she caught him staring at her or was she caught staring at him? She quickly lowered her gaze and looked outside, smiling.

"What's funny?" he asked.

"I have just remembered something, and it seemed like a déjà vu."

"What would that be, mysterious woman?"

"Just the way you hold the steering."

"What about it?" he asked, chuckling under his breath.

"Like you are caressing it passionately," she blurted out and cursed.

He threw his head back and laughed out before his car swerved. The car behind them honked, and he concentrated on his driving for a while before resuming their conversation.

"The way you look at me is so wanting," she continued.

"But I have made it no secret to you. I want you. Ever since the first day we met." He glanced at her.

"You want me in what way?" she dared to ask.

"In every way, a man wants a woman."

"I don't understand," she said, blushing when he looked her way. What was he driving at?

"I want to be close to you, to make you happy and live happily ever after," he said thoughtfully.

She believed him.

"Does what you want include sex?" she asked, not knowing why.

"Tough questions, huh? I feel like I am being grilled for some top government position," he said, smiling, and if she hadn't known him so well, she could have thought he was serious.

"Just curious, that's all," she said, shrugging her shoulders and looking out the window.

Adams knew that she was looking forward to his answer. She cared more about his reply than she let on.

"Yes. I want sex too," he said, startling her from her reverie.

"Ooh," was all she managed to say, not quite believing him.

He reached for her hand and liked its feel in his—so small, delicate, and painted a shade of royal blue.

There was an undeniable flow of irresistible force, and when their eyes met, it was like the mating of souls. He withdrew his hand to continue with his driving.

"I thought that you were different," she teased.

"I am not a monk. I am a red-blooded Black man attracted to an incredibly beautiful and intelligent woman."

"Good to know," she feigned disinterest.

Since that meeting with David, something had changed in her, but she still hadn't figured it out. One thing for sure was that, while she was beating herself about the heartbreak and harbouring bitterness, David was not. In fact, he had been enjoying his life in the arms of his new wife. Too busy to bother with her. It was like twisting a hot knife through her heart.

It was high time she gave herself a chance with Adams to see how things turned out. If he kept doing what he was doing, they would certainly be fine.

"C'mon, don't tell me you are a nun," he probed.

"No, I'm not, but that doesn't mean I want to jump your bones," she said, wrinkling her nose.

"Feel free to jump my bones anytime you want," he urged her, and they laughed.

They arrived at the Mahi Mahiu winding paths, exploring the beautiful landscape. She inhaled deeply, enjoying the view of the hills and surrounding valley.

It reminded her so much of her life. The twists and turns, the peaks and the lows. Yet despite all these absurdities, life was still beautiful, precious, and worth living.

The road finally brought them to Bogoria, where they took the rough road. They drove for twenty minutes before getting to their destination. When the car stopped, she jumped out of the car to survey her surroundings. Trees and tents covered the land. The environment was quiet and serene, with the only sounds of birds singing.

Adams went to stand by her and asked, "What do you think?"

"It is lovely," she said, reaching for his hand.

CHAPTER TWENTY-FIVE

Akinyi got into the warm water and felt her muscles unclenching under the therapeutical effect of the water. She swam the short distance to where Adams was waiting with his arms wide open. She went into them, and he encased her in a tight embrace. Around them were three couples who were too engrossed in each other to pay them any attention. After greetings, they ignored them for most of the night, not that Adams and Akinyi cared. In fact, that was even better. Everybody minded their own business.

"How are you feeling? Cold?" Adams asked, tracing his finger on her palm.

She shuddered.

"No, I'm feeling hot. This water feels heavenly."

"You look hot too," Adams said, holding her gaze in the candlelight.

The moon and the stars above them accentuated his chiselled body even more. The water reflected in his eyes, making them look glassy, intense, and mysterious.

She swallowed, affected by the intensity of everything, being in his arms, his proximity, his musky scent.

"Thanks," she said and quickly turned away when she saw the naked lust reflected in his eyes.

She felt like giving herself to him. And she wondered what triggered that feeling. Was it that they were out here in the wild with the moon and stars as witnesses to what they felt? Maybe it was the mystery of the darkness. The mood was right, and it would pass with time.

"Is that the Orion?" Akinyi asked, looking up.

She needed something to distract her mind from images of their tangled, sweaty bodies.

"I don't know. When the teacher was teaching the topic, I was absent from school."

"You don't strike me as a truant."

"I used to be. My friends and I used to skip school when the rivers swelled to swim and watch naked girls bathing."

"And you found that better than staying in school and listening to boring lessons?" She giggled.

"Of course, we were young boys who were very curious about life. The day my father found out, he beat the shit out of me."

"How did he find out?" she asked, amused.

"The class teacher wrote him a letter, and when he checked the blank pages in my book, it confirmed his worst fears."

"So, did the whipping help?"

"A little, but it was the ultimatum that did the magic. It was either I went to school or moved out.

I was only in class seven and not a shilling to my name. It wasn't much of a choice."

"I think I like your father already," she said.

Sadness clouded Adams. He missed his father and wondered if the ice around his heart had thawed?

Then again, how could his family blame him for Mother's death? If he'd known his parent had been depressed, he would have returned home. But nobody had told him. So it was unfair for them to rest the entire blame on him.

Akinyi saw the dismay in Adams' expression.

Did he have a fallout with his father? It seemed his family was still a sore topic. Would he ever forgive them? Would they ever reunite?

"Show me the cave?" Akinyi asked to cheer him up and saw relief wash over his expression.

"Why not!" he said as they started swimming towards the cave. However, it was very dark, and she couldn't find the courage to go in. He emerged from the cave after a minute of waiting.

"It looks scary and dark."

"C'mon, don't chicken out on me."

"Hold my hand then."

He took her hand and led her into the could barely make out his frame, although his breath fanned her face. The space was so small that their bodies crushed together.

"What are you thinking?" she asked after a beat.

"You," he responded hoarsely, his breathing becoming ragged by the minute.

What was it about confined spaces and increased chemistry? He felt close to her in ways he had never dared to entangle with a woman unless he would make love to her.

He tugged her near, crushing her body to his, limb to limb.

Their breaths marching, she felt so in tune with him, her entire body tingling with desire. His dick poked her stomach, strong, thick. Her core throbbed in response, wanting to welcome it to her warmth, her softness.

She dared not move, holding herself stiff, wondering whether to take it in her palm and rub it or let him lead wherever he wanted this to go.

Indecision warred within her. She thanked her lucky stars because it was dark, and he couldn't see her body's response, begging to be taken and pleasured.

She coughed to clear her throat. "Adams?"

"Yes. Are you OK?" he answered hoarsely.

"I don't know."

He chuckled.

"Sorry, there is just something about being in the cave at night, just the two of us. My body is betraying me. Does it affect you?" he asked.

"I don't know," she said after a while.

"What do you know then?" he asked.

"That you want to have sex with me."

He laughed softly at her bluntness. "That I want, but at the right time, not now."

"Ooh, you seem so sure of getting it."

"I have no doubt about that. Trust me, we will collide. But I will only do it when you are ready and begging for it."

"Begging?" she asked with a smirk on her face.

"Trust me, you will beg, and I won't gratify you immediately. Instead, I will drive you fast and hard to the brink, and my name will be a mantra on your lips."

She shivered from thinking about it. How could he make her so wanton by just saying the most indecent things to her?

"That remains to be seen," she said, brushing her body provocatively on his, and she heard him hiss. Was she playing too close to the cliff?

"Don't do that? I am so tight like a rubber band I can snap at any time unless you want me to take you now when we both know you are not ready."

"How do you know I am not ready?" She asked, her insides clenching. If only he touched her down there, he'd know that she was more than ready to move things along.

"That's my secret. When you are, I will know."

"Mr Know-it-all, let's go sleep."

They got out of the cave, and the area was deserted. Everyone had gone to bed. The night air had become so cold that they shivered as they made their way out of the water.

They hurried to their tents to prevent the cold from seeping into their bones. They changed into nightwear and climbed into the small sleeping mat. Their bodies touched despite their attempt to keep a safe distance between themselves.

When Akinyi heard his regular breathing, she assumed he was asleep. She turned to look at him and found his eyes wide open staring at her.

"What! I thought you were asleep," she exclaimed.

"I'm trying to, but my thoughts are scattered." He shifted and lay on his side.

"What are you thinking about?"

"Taking you into my arms and holding you as you sleep,"

"Then what's stopping you?"

He smiled, pulling her into his arms, and she went willingly. She laid her head on his chest, and he encircled her safely in his arms. She had never felt this safe and cared for.

She shifted, trying to get comfortable and snuggling close to him. He just held her as sleep took him.

***

"Good morning," Adams greeted with a smile.

Akinyi stretched, opening her eyes. She mumbled a reply as she sat up.

He just watched her keenly. He had observed her as she slept and fell in love with her a hundred folds over. She was so beautiful that it hurt looking at her, and now that she was awake, she looked even more attractive.

"Do you know that looking at a woman like that is morally repugnant?" she said, stifling a yawn.

He smiled, chuckling under his breath. If only she had an inkling of what he had been thinking about…

"Let's go make breakfast. With the way you are yawning, you could eat a goat." He climbed out of the tent.

"Wrong. I could eat two goats," she countered, and he laughed.

They made breakfast on the tri-stone fireplace and drank tea while sitting under a tree.

"I like the primitiveness of this place. It's living with only the basic necessities, no luxuries. Like the early man." She sipped her tea.

"With the exception that we are wearing clothes and not walking naked." He winked at her.

"But they used to wear animal skins,"

"I agree, but that was just the other day. The earliest African men used to walk naked with some skin around the front to cover their private parts. So, if someone was coming from your front, you covered your fundamentals. if they were approaching from behind, you shift it to cover your behind."

"What if they are coming from the front and behind?" she asked, no longer able to contain her laughter.

"Then I guess you choose which part is more private than the other and cover it." He tapped his fingers.

"For you, which part would you cover?" She pointed to him.

"Oh, Akinyi, I'm not an early man."

"Stop evading the question." Soaking her bread in tea before taking a bite.

"In which case, I guess I will cover my behind." He chuckled and liked the surprised look on her face.

"And walk around swinging your stuff? Where will the women place their eyes as they approach you?" Incredulous, she crossed her arms over her chest.

"Wherever they like. It's not like they will take anything from it by looking. I know most will avert their eyes. Others will even jump and hide in the bush."

"Such a mannerless man you would have been." She waved him away.

"Maybe that's why God saw it fit to place me in this modern era. What about you? Where would you cover?"

"I would make leaves to cover my breasts and others to cover my behind and put that skin on the front."

"Ooh, that would kill the fun for the young men who want to observe."

"Well, they will have to focus their observant eyes on the other girls. You would have ogled me until your eyes pierced my leaves and animal skin."

Adams chuckled. "What makes you say that?"

"I have seen how you look at me even with my clothes on. I wonder what would happen if I only had the flimsy leaves around my fundamentals or, worse yet, no covering."

Adams laughed at her insinuation. "From now onwards, I will never look at you. I will close my eyes every time I'm around you."

"Then how will you get around with your eyes closed." Her forehead creased in thought.

"By feeling my way with my hands." He demonstrated, feeling the air.

"Ooh, that's an excuse to touch me. I suggest you keep your eyes open." She smiled.

He nodded in agreement.

"Let's go explore the caves around here before the sun gets too hot," he suggested.

Akinyi changed into her pair of brown shorts and a body-hugging white t-shirt. He was in black track trousers and a navy-blue t-shirt. By the time they started their hike, it was thirty minutes past eight. The sun was just beginning to warm the earth.

They crossed the stream feeding their natural spa and climbed two small slopes, ending at a small cave. Humongous spiders and scorpions crawled out of it to bask in the sun. Fascinated, they watched as more creepy-crawlies crept out.

After a while, they moved on, exploring other caves not too far from the first one. One seemed bare of creatures, so they went inside.

She ran her fingers along the rough surfaces, excitement buzzing through her.

"Can we play hide and seek?" she suggested.

"No, we are too old for that," he admonished.

"I feel like I am sweet sixteen, and I can imagine you being sweet seventeen," she teased.

The doe eye she gave him made her appear like an innocent sixteen-year-old.

"Ahh, my sweet-sixteen girl, run and hide," he said and liked the playful glee that brightened her face. He wanted to always see her happy and know that he was the cause of it.

"Brikicho," he called out, closing his eyes.

"Banture," she responded, looking for a hiding place.

After a while, she stopped responding, and he took it as a cue to start his search. He looked inside the caves and saw no sign of her.

"Please come out, Sexy Back," he called out to her.

He scratched his head, getting exasperated when he remembered one place he hadn't searched. Finally, he rounded the cave and found her squatting between boulders.

"Catch you!" he shouted, and she stood up frowning. "Shouldn't I be rewarded?"

He lifted her by the waist, swinging her around.

Surprised, she squealed, breath coming out in gasps.

Lowering her to the ground, he examined her worriedly. "Are you alright?"

"Yes, I was just a little dizzy from the swinging." She exhaled steadily. "What kind of reward do you have in mind?"

"Surprise me." His eyes darkened with want.

She hugged him for less than five seconds and stood back.

"After searching for so long, a one-second hug is all you can offer?" he asked, winking at her.

He looked so attractive right now. Her mouth dried out.

"Learn to appreciate the little you get, so you will also be able to get plenty in future."

"That's one of the notions that pastors use to delude the believers that their riches are in Heaven. I'm not a believer in the future that is not even guaranteed. I believe in having it all in the present,"

"Ooh. Sorry to disappoint you, but that is all I can offer now."

His eyes brimmed with a challenge, but she shrugged in a devil-may-care way.

"What if I give you a lift back to the pool? Will I receive a better reward?"

"Definitely, my dear Adams, but you left your car."

"I will carry you on my back," he said, motioning for her to climb on.

"And have the villagers laughing at a grown woman carried on the back, no thanks," she replied, shaking her head.

"It is good that they don't know who we are then," he countered.

She considered the situation for a while before climbing onto his back. Although she felt more like a child than the woman she was supposed to be, she was tired of minding other people's opinions and acting decently to avoid being the centre of gossip.

"Are you good to go?" he asked after she wound her hands securely around his neck.

"Yes," she confirmed, feeling on top of the world.

He straightened and walked towards their camp. He held her legs to keep her in place, his fingers clamped on her bare skin.

Adams cursed himself for proposing the lift.

Her front brushed his back provocatively, making him aware of her—her soft breasts caressing his back and the fast drumming of her heartbeats thrumming through him.

Oh, the things he could do to this woman...

When they arrived at the stream, he was glad that the torment was over. Ready to receive his reward, he lowered her and flexed his taut muscles.

"Thanks for the lift. It was quite an experience," she said, stretching too.

"The pleasure was all mine. Where is my reward?" No need to beat about the bush.

"I will cook you a very delicious lunch," she said, smiling sweetly when she saw the frown lines marring on his face.

"Then get working," he said, at last, resigned to his fate.

"What's wrong? Not the kind of reward you expected?"

"You are right. I expected something up close and personal,"

"Isn't cooking up close and personal?"

"Not by a long shot because both of us are going to eat,"

"Selfish man. I wonder what you had in mind. Something that would particularly please only you."

"Wonder no more, Jaber," he said, his voice husky.

He held her eyes riveted to his, and he moved purposefully forward with that devilish smile spread across his face. She just stood in awe, waiting for him to do with her as he pleased.

He leaned his forehead on hers before claiming her mouth possessively.

She opened to him, a willing accomplice to his harsh mouth. What was the need of resisting this when it was what she wanted? She matched his vigour.

When he pulled back to look at her, he was surprised by the desire clearly written on her face. Her eyes shone with need, lips parted, and breathing ragged. Yet there was something else. She was no longer resisting him. In fact, she was very receptive.

He had noticed the change once but ignored it as his overactive imagination. Now, he was sure. He kissed her again to confirm and felt her wildness. The flicker of light at the end of the tunnel. He just had to play his cards well. It wasn't his intention to scare her away now that he had gained her trust.

When he pulled back a second time, she looked away, embarrassed. "After that kiss, you expect me to still cook your lunch?"

"Of course. We both benefitted from the kiss, remember," he countered.

She narrowed her eyes in disbelief. "But who benefitted more?"

"You, of course. I wish we had a camera to capture the moment," he said.

She smiled, knowing that it was the truth. He was a good kisser. She would give him that. And she wondered how he would make love? Was he wild or mild? She quickly left to go prepare lunch. She dared not look at him with the path her mind had taken.

Adams walked away, needing space to clear his troubled mind. He wandered to the stream and sat on a big rock facing the water, and willed his brain to go blank. He closed his eyes, listening to the gurgling water, the cool breeze on his face.

Thoughts of the army came forth. The happy moments when they had subdued the enemies, the quiet nights on patrol when they observed the starry skies wishing they were home. However, they had always managed to keep such thoughts at bay with laughter, alcohol, and women. The combination was toxic enough to keep at bay the loneliness and emptiness gnawing at their souls. But somehow, he wanted to only remember the good.

His mind shifted to his life after retirement from the army. His civilian agemates were already married with children. Once again, he was reminded of how different his life had spanned out. Lonely. At the end of the day, it was nice to go home to someone, to love. The empty echo of the house, coldness and silence weren't intriguing companions.

He had never thought about how much a family impacted a person's life. Then he met Akinyi, and being with her was more addictive than he had anticipated. Sometimes he wondered how he had managed to live all this while without her. It was true what they said that 'you never know what you are missing until it arrives.'

His mind somehow kept playing the last episode with Akinyi so many times. Was it possible? He didn't want to ask her because he knew she would deny it. Or was he afraid that he could be wrong? Or that if he brought it to her knowledge, she would raise her guards up? He didn't know which reason was overriding the others, but he wanted to keep it to himself. He was hoping that he was right.

CHAPTER TWENTY-SIX

Akinyi strolled to the stream when she finished cooking and found Adams looking lost in thought.

She could have sworn she heard his brain wheels grinding. She walked to him and blindfolded him with her hands, and his lips turned up in a smile.

"Aswito, or are you my Bungoma wheelbarrow?" he asked as she removed her hands from his eyes.

"Whichever suits your mood."

"I'm spoilt for choice."

He grinned, and she stepped in front of him.

"Are you hungry yet?"

"I am famished."

He trailed his gaze from her exposed legs to linger on her breasts covered by the t-shirt.

Heat rose from her toes to her head, rushing down and settling on her stomach. His hungry eyes devoured her. Were they still talking about food?

"Then get your butt off that rock and follow me," she said, feigning innocence.

"Are you sure about this?" he asked, his eyes hooded, unreadable as his Adam's apple bobbed.

"Of course, I am talking about the food I just cooked," she whispered and smiled.

Grinning, he stood and followed her to the makeshift kitchen. She served their food on plates, and they went to the eating area.

He sighed and closed his eyes when he tasted the food. "This is very delicious."

"You are exaggerating."

"I'm serious. Now I understand why they say whoever has a wife is king."

"Mmmh, suit yourself," she said, not wanting to argue that she was not his wife.

The glow in his eyes was contagious, and she didn't want to spoil the moment. Deep down in her heart, she knew that she wanted to make this man happy. She wanted him to look at her with wonder in his eyes, just like he was doing now.

"Eat your food," he said.

She was nibbling at her food and moving the food on her plate from one corner to the other. She resumed her eating, her appetite gone. Staring at him, he cleared his plate of food and gobbled down her food. Once she removed her plates, they sat for a while chatting before they went swimming.

The water caressed their bodies, its warmth soothing. The other couples were also in the water, and they were playing with the ball throwing it back and forth. They joined them. The ball was thrown from one end to the other by one group while the other group was in the middle of the water trying to catch the ball. The throwing group had to throw the ball higher to prevent them from catching it. Adams and Akinyi joined separate groups. The game continued for a while as laughter and shouts filled the air. Adams' group won the game because it comprised tall people who were pros at jumping and catching the ball.

The next game was that of diving. One group stood in a straight line and kept their legs wide apart while the other group dived and passed between their legs until they came to the other end. Some people like Akinyi, who couldn't hold their breaths for long, only managed to pass through two or three people before coming above the water. Adams managed to come out after the tenth person, and everyone clapped for him. They finished the game after a while and people scattered in different directions. Most people left the water, and those who remained were coupled up in separate spots.

Adams urged Akinyi to hop onto his back, and he swam them to the spot near the cave. "I have missed you," he whispered in her ears once they reached their place, his two-day-old beard tickling her neck.

She squirmed. "But we were together during the game."

He propped his back on a rock while her back leaned against his front, and he wrapped arms around her

"We were in different groups. It's true that absence makes the heart grow fonder."

"Are you a philosopher now?" she asked curiously.

"It depends. There is a saying that if you find a good wife, you will be happy, but if you find a bad one, you will become a philosopher,"

"Ooh. Are you insinuating that I'm a bad wife?" She narrowed her eyes.

"Not really. Can we go into the cave while it's still daylight?" he asked, sidestepping the question.

She nodded, and they proceeded into the cave, stopping briefly under the gentle, cascading waterfall, letting the water caress their backs.

Adams then led the way into the cave. His back was on the cave wall while she stood inches from him, facing him. Water seeped through the rocks blinding her.

He tugged her out of the water, crushing her body against his, making her tingle everywhere they connected.

Her breath hitched, and she smiled weakly, nervously. At least the other night, they were covered in darkness, and he could not tell just how affected she was by their proximity.

He regarded her intently. She burned under the gaze. With his arms around her waist, she couldn't escape before the inevitable happened.

But again, it was high time it happened to get it out of their system. She wasn't in this alone. She'd developed a profound respect for him for not taking advantage. He had been kind to her and had won her trust and heart little by little. He was not Team Mafisi, indeed.

She looked at his mouth, and her eyes quickly flew to his eyes which were now dark and hooded, giving her a chance to move things along or end them. It gave her power. The next step was in her hands. Would she step up or walk away? She planted a light kiss on his right cheek catching him by surprise, his skin warm, his beards rough. She was en route to kiss the other cheek when he quickly captured her mouth with his. Impatient man, she thought, opening for him, letting his tongue glide into her mouth, his sweet breath making her want the kiss to last forever.

His hands started roaming her body. She stilled, stood stiff. He pulled away to look at her.

"What's wrong?" he asked, caressing her cheeks, and she closed her eyes, leaning into his hands.

"Nothing, Adams," she whispered, meeting his gaze.

"Are you afraid?" he probed.

"I will be if you continue talking," she teased, giving him a shut-up kiss, and he continued kissing her, exploring her mouth. His hands wandered from her back to her breasts, and he caressed them, taking them into his hands, and they fitted perfectly. This elicited a moan from her, but he didn't stop. She didn't want him to stop, pushing into his hands.

"Adams, please," she whispered urgently.

"Please what, Sexy Back?" he asked hoarsely, rising to look at her, and she almost shouted in frustration because she didn't want him to stop.

His wicked smile indicated he knew exactly what he was doing. "I told you that you will beg,"

"Don't be so full of yourself," she murmured, lowering her gaze, and he cursed, tilting her chin so that she could look at him.

"Sorry about that," he said softly, remorse in his eyes.

How could she stay mad at him? She was still lost in her thoughts when his hands reached her shoulder to lower her swimming costume. She didn't move. She just looked into his eyes, not speaking. But words were a waste.

Her outfit fell to her waist, exposing her upright boobs and his eyes left hers to look at them. She heard his sharp intake of breath before his eyes rose again to meet hers. She saw fire in his eyes. Was this passion overdrive?

"You are so beautiful," he murmured, taking one of her nipples into his warm mouth, flicking his tongue, suckling. Alternating to the right one, he lightly bit on her nipple before soothing it with his tongue as he pleasured her breasts with both his hands and mouth.

Her climax washed over her body, and she felt her knees weakening, but he held her firmly, not letting go. When she regained her consciousness, she looked at him and saw a satisfied grin on his face. She covered her face with her hands. She could not believe that he had seen her at her weakest point. What would he think of her now?

"Stop overthinking, baby. I loved watching you climax, so real and original," he said, removing her hands from her face.

She wondered how he could bring her to climax with just a kiss and still sound perfectly fine. Maybe he was unaffected by her. Her eyes travelled lower and widened in surprise by how much he had grown, straining against his pair of swimming shorts. This was unfair. How comes she was feeling so satiated while he clearly wasn't?

"Don't worry about me," he said, smiling when she frowned.

"Why shouldn't I?" she asked, adjusting her costume, and he reached out to help her.

"I will be fine. Just give me some time to cool down." He caressed her arm, and she nodded.

Scooping a handful of water, she poured it on her hot skin. After a few minutes, they left the cave, and she was surprised that it was already dark. The other couples had returned and were involved in actions of their own. Some were kissing ferociously. Others were holding each other as if their lives depended on it.

Akinyi smiled knowingly as they got out of the water. They walked to their tent in companionable silence, matching steps. He reached out to hold her hand, and it felt like the most natural thing in the world. They towelled themselves and wore their dry clothes. They then sat on one of the benches looking at the sky.

Akinyi felt like staying here forever with this man, this moment, and this night. That was the only thing she wanted from Fate, and she hoped she would be granted that simple plea.

Adams was also lost in his own private thoughts. This woman was absolutely amazing. She was beautiful and intelligent, and her response to his ministration surpassed his wildest dreams. Pleasing her was enough, even if he didn't get his own gratification. He wanted to do it again and again.

"What's on your mind, baby?"

"Now my name has changed from Sexy Back to baby, interesting,"

"They change according to the mood. Right now, you are my baby," he clarified, giving her the bedroom gaze that had been her undoing ever since she set eyes on him.

"I was just thinking about this night?"

"It's beautiful, huh?"

"Yeah, and I am just sitting here in the middle of nowhere with this handsome man. And I feel satisfied. Life is just complete. Such a strange feeling."

He didn't rush in to fill the silence that followed, and she was relieved. He wasn't one to talk just for the sake. Instead, he allowed others to talk their hearts out and absorbed everything before speaking. This made her feel like he really understood her deeply. It made her admire him even more.

The silence brought forth other sounds around them. The crickets were chirping, and the wind was blowing softly, making the leaves sway leisurely like they were engaged in a Rhumba dance. He pulled her to him, holding her close. The heat from his body seeped into her, warming her, taking over her. He let her sleep for a while before waking her.

"I thought we could go back into the water after supper," he said when she was fully awake.

"I don't know. I am just tired. Maybe tomorrow," she apologized, her eyes pleading for understanding. The orgasms he had given her had worn her out. She just wanted to rest.

Adams nodded. They warmed the leftover lunch meal and ate quickly. Afterwards, they cleared up and went to the tent. She changed into her blue nightdress and lay down. Adams, who had excused himself, came back and lay next to her. She had felt tired while outside, but sleep eluded her now that she was next to him. All her senses were alert, so aware of him even though she had her back to him.

She had always held herself aloof because of David. However, she wasn't blind to the undercurrent brewing between her and Adams. They both wanted it. She was tired of denying this attraction. She should stop fighting it and see where it would lead them.

She turned to face him. She didn't want to wait any longer. He was beginning to doze off, she nudged him softly, and he opened his eyes. The moon was high up in the sky, illuminating the tent.

"Hey, are you ok?"

"Yes," she whispered, moving closer to him. She caressed his head and kissed him on the lips. He responded wildly, pulling her on top of him and holding her close, but still, it wasn't enough. Tonight, there was something in her.

They kissed for a while, their hand caressing, their tongues exploring. He pulled up her nightie and caressed her thighs, butt and back.

Finally, he removed the dress and pulled her legs astride him so that she was directly on top of him, grazing his dick. She felt the blunt tip of his hard-on, poking her, searching for her core, and rubbed herself on him, his groans spurring her on.

She wanted to feel his skin against hers. She helped him out of his shirt. She then pushed his shorts and boxers lower. His erection sprang free, long and proud. She reached out, feeling its throbbing, heavy weight in her hands. She swallowed, desire swirling in her pussy, making her wet with need.

He quickly helped her out of her panties, balling them in his hands before inhaling, closing his eyes. She whimpered as he swiped his index finger on her pussy, lightly pinching her swollen clit before pausing at her entrance. She couldn't take it anymore. She rubbed on his hand, wanting his finger deep inside her. He chuckled and held her gaze, his eyes mirroring his desire.

"Akinyi," he growled, pushing his fingers through, filling her, and she squeezed her thighs to lock him in place and keep him there. Forever wasn't long enough. He stalled, and she swore that his eyes darkened, even more, savouring this connection between their bodies. Parting her legs, he added another finger, rubbing her tender depth, in and out, grazing her sweet spot.

"Aah. Adams!" she called, canting her hips, keeping up with him, her body on fire.

"You feel so warm…so soft, and I can't wait to sink into you," he whispered hoarsely, increasing his pace, adding a third finger, bringing her to the edge faster.

A sheen of sweat formed on her body, and he rubbed faster until she finally came, moaning against his shoulder. She was so wet and so ready for him.

He flipped her under him and loomed on top, kissing her tenderly.

She caressed his back, holding him tightly.

"Akinyi," he murmured her name, moving lower to explore her body, his warm breath and coarse feel of his beard making her shudder. His heat spread on her body wherever their bodies touched. He took one of her nipples and sucked it while he caressed the other until she was now a whimpering, squirming mess.

"Adams, please…" she whispered, but he didn't stop. Instead, he moved lower, kissing, blowing on her skin, tickling her with his beard. He kissed her belly button. She was shivering with want and needed him to claim her and end her sweet misery.

She wasn't prepared for his mouth when he blew warm air on her hot pussy. Without warning, he took her in his mouth. Her breath caught, and before she could resist, he was circling his tongue and gently sucking on her clit. She held his head in place when flashes of warmth and cold licked up her body.

Unrelenting, his tongue flicked in and out her opening, his gaze holding hers, and it was so intense that her toes curled as she fisted the sheets to hold onto her balance. Finally, he sheathed himself before claiming her when she thought she could not take it anymore. His blunt tip nudging her wet, welcoming entrance, pushing in, filling her completely. He stayed like that for a while, letting them savour the moment. When he started moving above her, she moaned and caressed his back. His eyes were locked on hers all the time, mirroring every emotion.

She reached out and caressed his face as she started to move her hips in circles, meeting him halfway. He pumped in and out, matching her pace, a dance between the sheets. After a while, his body was glistening with sweat. He was perfect. The thought propelled her into climax. He increased the pace until he groaned her name as he poured himself into her, his heart beating fast against her breast.

He was about to move to his side when she held him in place, still joined. She felt him still throbbing in her. He kissed her deeply, and she tightened her hold on him.

He looked at her, a smile spreading across his face. "Damn! Woman, I want to make love to you repeatedly until we are too tired to go on."

She nodded. "I would really love that."

She wondered why she had taken this long again before engaging in this. She was done waiting and wanted to live each day as it came. No more holding back.

He rolled to his side, excusing himself to dispose of the latex. When he returned, he spooned her body, and they slept in each other's arms. They woke up sometime before 5 o'clock, resuming their kissing like they hadn't stopped.

"Let's go to the water," he whispered, and she nodded. So they walked the short distance to the water holding hands. The pool was warm, and it quickly chased away the morning chill. He immediately pulled her to him. They kissed under the moon and the stars.

Adams knelt on one of the stones at the edge and whispered, "Please marry me, Akinyi."

Akinyi opened her mouth and closed it again, but no words spilled out. Instead, she looked into his eyes glowing in the moonlight, the ring glittering in his hand. Was it too early in the morning to receive a marriage proposal?

"Just say yes," he pleaded, tugging at her hand. This man had been nothing but good to her, treated her like a true lady. Although he had been a man in uniform, he was an honourable man.

She glided to him and put her arms around him, and whispered in his ears, "Yes, I will gladly marry you."

His face broke into the widest grin she had ever seen. He slipped the ring on her finger and lifted her high up. She could help the laughter that escaped her mouth and filled the morning air. When he claimed her mouth again, she knew with certainty that he was the man for her. He made love to her in the water, her legs wrapped against his waist, and she threw back her head and moaned as he took her to places she had never been.

***

They spent two more days at Bogoria in each other's arms, making love, swimming, and making more love. They were insatiable. They arrived at their home in the evening, so tired that they ate their meal fast.

Akinyi felt happy that she was his wife in reality. She understood that sometimes good things fall apart so that better things can fall together.

"Can we retire to bed now?" Adams asked, getting up. Akinyi stifled a yawn as she nodded.

CHAPTER TWENTY-SEVEN

Adams returned home from the farm tired. He wanted to take a quick bath and start dinner before Akinyi returned.

Weeks had passed since their time in Bogoria, and they were expecting their first child. Akinyi had let Mama Awino go. But she'd given her a better position at the Child Protection Office as an advocate for children's rights.

When Adams had asked, Akinyi had said that she wanted to look after her husband on her own.

He'd chuckled, hugging her tightly. "Take care of me, Akinyi."

"I intend to, my love." She'd kissed him thoroughly.

Now, he went to the fridge to retrieve water when the doorbell rang. Thinking his wife was returning early, he hurried to the door and swung it open.

He froze, mouth dropping open.

Linda, his ex, stared at him, smiling broadly, and she jumped forward, hugging his neck. He stood unmoving, and Linda pulled away to look at him, a curious light in her eyes.

"What are you doing here?" he asked, his voice dripping with cold as he crossed his arms on his chest.

"Honey, is that the way to treat your mistress?" she asked seductively, dressed in a short black dress, showing off her thighs.

Memories of their wild sex flashed in his mind, and he hardened briefly, the unwanted sensation swiftly chased by the heat of shame at his reaction.

Linda saw his indecision and waltzed into the house. She made herself comfortable on the couch, her thighs open.

He averted his gaze, went to the opposite chair and sat down.

"Linda, listen..." he said, trying to get the words out as she crossed and uncrossed her legs.

"You need to get out of here," he summoned. She had to leave before Akinyi returned.

But Linda wasn't listening to anything he was saying. Instead, she was playing with her tits, looking at him. Then she moved next to him on the couch, and he cursed under his breath.

"Do you mean that, honey?" she asked, trying to kiss his face.

Before he could shove her away, the front door opened, and Akinyi stood there, glaring at them. Then she turned around and slammed the door behind her.

Adams quickly pushed Linda, who laughed as she adjusted her dress.

"Get out of here now!" Adams thundered.

When she sat back on her seat, still grinning, he stood up, pulled her out of her chair, and pushed her out the door.

"Sorry, Adams. You should have told me you are married. But I have no money. Give me some, and I promise never to disturb you," Linda pleaded.

Adams quickly removed his wallet and gave her two thousand shillings. She took the money and walked away, swinging her bag merrily. Adams watched as she disappeared and shook his head. The past was always bound to come knocking.

He then found Akinyi sitting on the porch, staring at the horizon. She was immobile as a statue with two flowing fountains. Her face was sad, and tears flowed freely down her cheeks and made the front of her dress soak.

Guilt ate at him. Pain radiated in his chest, seeing her like this and knowing he was the cause. He had always wanted to bring her happiness. He wondered what was going through her mind. Was she ever going to forgive him?

He was still thinking of what to do when she moved her head to face him. He expected her to shout and throw things at him like most women do. But she did none of those. Her eyes held a pained look, and he longed to hold her and comfort her. Maybe it would have been better if she had shouted because he would have known what she was thinking. Perhaps he would have managed to break the impenetrable wall and reach out to her and beg for her forgiveness

She rose from her seat softly and staggered into the house. He moved to follow her, but she raised her hand to stop him. He went to the chair she had vacated and sat down. He stayed out until darkness descended on Kachieng'. He had to make her understand that he only desired one woman—her. What she had seen meant nothing and would never happen again.

He flicked the lights in the sitting room and walked to the bedroom, where he found her curled in the furthest corner of the bed, facing away from him. He climbed the bed, moved closer to her, and held her. She didn't resist him, and he held on to her tightly. She had stopped crying now and would heave every now and then.

He gently turned her so that she was facing him.

"Why?" she mouthed.

"I am so sorry, my love. It wasn't what it seemed," he said, wiping her tear-streaked cheeks.

She looked at him with raised brows, and he knew he had to come clean about everything.

"Her name is Linda. She was my mistress. We had been together for about fourteen years. I guess she hasn't seen me for long and came to seek me out. But I have no desire to go to her, believe me."

"Really? But when I walked in, it didn't seem so. You were more than willing to make love to her in our matrimonial home!" she said, her voice rising.

"No, I wasn't! I am sorry. I was sending her away when you came in. She was trying to be persistent," he said, and she eyed him angrily, pulling out of his hold and storming to the bathroom. He wanted to follow her but didn't know what he would say to assuage her pain. So he remained seated on the bed. The shower was running, and he could hear her sobbing. He felt lost.

"My love, please let me in," he knocked on the door. When she didn't answer, he turned the knob and found the door unlocked. He saw her sitting under the sprinkling water, all wet and shivering. He walked to the shower and turned it off. He carried her back to the bedroom as water dripped on the floor, forming a trail and soaking his front.

He helped her change into dry clothes. When he put her to bed, she was still shivering and heaving. All this was not good for her or the baby. She had to eat too. He went to the kitchen and came back with food. She shook her head when he asked her to eat.

"Don't do this!" he shouted in frustration, putting the food away.

"Do what? Cry? I am sad that my husband was fooling with another woman on the couch. I should have followed my instincts. No good can come from marrying a man in uniform," she said, throwing arrows at his tender heart.

Adams shook his head in disbelief. "What has this got to do with me being a man in uniform?"

"I should have learned my lesson a long time ago," she snarled, driving the arrows, piercing his heart, wanting him to hurt.

He flinched. She had probably touched a chord, just as she had intended. She rubbed her face, tilting her face to the ceiling, the pain in her heart unbearable, nonetheless.

"Really, Akinyi! You are not fair." He glared at her.

She shrugged, not wanting to continue with this conversation. She was bound to say hurtful words that would cause irreparable scars. Reaching for her food, she gobbled it down, the meal tasteless that she might as well have been eating leaves.

Adams noted that she would not say more on the topic, turned his back and lay down. Akinyi curled up on her side, fuming. Still, she felt sadness welling up inside her body underneath all the anger, racking it with its force. She tried to sob quietly, but it was impossible. Instead, her anguished cries filled their bedroom. Adams moved closer to her, snuggling.

"I am so sorry, my love." He caressed her, consoling her, whispering to her.

When her crying was reduced to sobs, she moved out of his embrace. He turned his back, probably giving up. The thought of him touching another woman had her stomach churning with jealousy. The nerve of that man! Maybe she would have caught them in the act if she had delayed returning home.

The thought made her shiver. She could tell that he was troubled with the tension between them. She knew she was supposed to feel happy for punishing him, punching him where it hurt the most, but she felt worse. Her last comment had been harsh, and she had seen how he had flinched and stopped trying to beg her.

She didn't want to go on like this. She wanted him to continue holding her close as she slept, rubbing her aching waist, and massaging her baby bump as he did every night. She stretched her hand to reach out to him but changed her mind. Instead, she turned to her side and tried to sleep.

When Akinyi woke up the following day, she was still livid. Adams' side of the bed was empty, cold. Walking out to the porch, she saw him repairing the fence at the far end of the field. He looked up from his work and waved at her unsmiling, and she waved back her hand heavy like the stone in her heart. She shuffled back to the house, bathed, took her breakfast, and left for the office. She was dragging and got to the office at 10. It was one of those mornings when no matter how fast she tried to move things along, they wouldn't gel.

The whole day she found herself thinking of yesternight. Had she been too hard on him? Now that the anger had faded away, she questioned whether he had intentionally set out to hurt her. She knew in her heart that could not be. He had said that the lady used to be his mistress, and she had even heard the lady ask him for money. Of course, he had a past before meeting her.

She then remembered her meeting with David at Ephy's place. Because of their past, she had almost given herself to David after a kiss. Yet they had only known each other for six years, while Adams had been with the mistress for fourteen years. For a moment, she got off her high horse. She kept on toying with her pen all morning. She could not work like this.

Adhiambo kept glancing at her with a worried expression. As much as the woman was her friend, she could not confide in her. If she did, everyone in the town would know about it before nightfall. It was just in Adhiambo's nature not to keep anything to herself, more like an itch she could not resist scratching.

Akinyi excused herself, walked to Grandma's place, and found her having tea with boiled yams.

"Welcome, Nyakwara." Grandma ushered her into the place, a smile turning up her lips.

Akinyi brought a second mug from the kitchen, and Grandma poured tea into it from an aluminium kettle. "How is your husband?"

"He is fine," Akinyi said too quickly, and Grandma looked up from her cup, her bright eyes reading her, piercing her.

Akinyi brought her tea to her lips, taking a long gulp, hiding behind her cup.

But there was nowhere to hide as the older woman studied her for several seconds before she broke eye contact and resumed munching her yam.

Akinyi sagged with relief on her seat.

"Spit out whatever is disturbing you."

"How do you know something is disturbing me?"

Grandma didn't answer and gave her that penetrative look again that sometimes gave Akinyi the creeps that she could read her innermost thoughts. Grandma was silent, daring her to deny it.

Knowing she would not win this battle, she told her everything that had happened. The old woman was quiet the whole time.

"Why didn't you forgive him when he asked for forgiveness?" the woman asked, pushing her plate away.

"I was angry, Grandma. I caught them!" She stood up, pacing the floor, a fresh bout of anger stirring within her.

Grandma dismissively waved her hand. "But he asked for your forgiveness. He is remorseful. Error is to be human. Sometimes, you need to be gentle with your husband."

Akinyi looked at the bundle of firewood next to the kitchen, suppressing the urge to walk out on her. As a woman? Was a woman to take all the rubbish that the husband brought? Maybe Grandma was from the ancient days and didn't understand the problems of the young generation.

As if reading her mind, she said, "You can go ahead and take what I say as hearsays. I have experience. I have been married to your grandfather for over sixty years. The problems experienced in marriage are more or less the same."

She reached for her worn-out dog-eared Bible, flipping the pages. "The bible says, 'woman respect your husband and husband love your wife'. This verse carries the entire secret to a successful marriage. You should be gentle with your husband. When he raises his voice, lower yours. It doesn't matter who is right. Like right now, you look like hell, and I am sure he is also miserable. How is that helping your marriage?"

Akinyi shrugged, taking her seat.

"Marriage is not a bed of roses, Nyakwara. You must learn to forgive one another. What if you become too harsh and drive him into the arms of another woman? You will start looking for whoever is bewitching your marriage, but you won't find it. Go home and make things right," Grandma concluded, rising.

Akinyi walked home, the words of Grandma echoing in her head throughout the journey. When she got there, she found Adams in the kitchen preparing dinner. The delicious smell of fried chicken wafted in the air, making her stomach grumble.

Adams turned to look at her hesitantly, studying her face, gauging if she was still angry at him. He startled when she closed the distance between them, putting her arms around his neck and kissing him full on the lips. His breath caught as he quickly put his arms around her waist and pulled her closer to him. They deepened the kiss, each taking as much as they could get. Then, Akinyi pulled one of her hands away from his neck and turned off the gas cooker. She dragged him to the bedroom, and he followed her, a sheepish grin on his face.

***

This was an unexpected twist, Adams mused, closing the bedroom door, shutting the world out. He didn't know what to expect when he woke up this morning. Akinyi had left for work pretty upset with him. After she left, he tried to busy himself with work around the ranch, feeding the cattle, and cutting grass. Still, he couldn't take his mind off her. He loved her so much and didn't want to lose her because of his stupid mistake. He was prepared to grovel if that was what it'd take to gain her forgiveness.

And then this. Oh God, this was a miracle. He was prepared to wear her out with multiple orgasms if that's what it took to be forgiven. She pushed him on the bed, the mattress dipping under his weight as he leaned his back on the pillow. She stood before him, shifting her weight from one foot to the next, biting her lower lip. He growled, his body warming up as blood rushed down to his member.

"Patience, Adams. Good things come to those who wait," her teasing sultry voice, a welcome relief.

"Akinyi, I'm ready to wait," he croaked, adjusting his now throbbing dick which tented his grey pants, making its presence and need known.

She smiled, amused as her heated gaze moved from his engorged dick. He was tempted to leap out of bed, bend her on all fours and lose himself inside her warmth. But this was her call. So he shifted on the bed.

She peeled off her clothes, one by one. First, the dress pooled at her feet, and she stepped out of it, then her bra and her panties. She did this in a slow, deliberate move, never taking her eyes away from his.

Adams looked at her perfect body, her steady breasts aching for his touch, her protruding stomach, which carried a manifestation of their love, her smooth thighs...

He followed suit and took his clothes off fast. First his shirt, jeans together with the boxer and then his sandals. She appraised him. The fading sun lit the room in yellow rays, making them look ethereal.

He walked to her and took her lips in his, pulling her warm, soft body close. God, he had missed holding her like this, feeling her body. Carrying her to the bed, he ran his hands and lips all over her body.

When they were ready, he entered her from behind, filling her completely, and she moaned his name. He thrust gently, prolonging it, making her body tremble, making her know that, for him, there never could be another.

When they climaxed, their dark shadows on the wall merged into one. He held her, raining kisses on her neck, her back. Then, turning her around to claim her lips, he professed his apology, love, desires and promises to be faithful to only her.

"Wow! Who can resist that?" she teased, framing his face. "The best make-up sex ever!" Pulling him close, holding him tight, accepting his apology.

His heart welled up with love for his woman, and he wanted to do right by her, always.

CHAPTER TWENTY-EIGHT

Akinyi played with the six-month-old Adams Junior on the carpeted sitting room floor when the doorbell rang. She picked up her son and went to the door. When she opened the door, her breath held.

An old man who was Adams' copyright, a younger man, and a young lady in her twenties stood there. Her in-laws.

Feeling giddy with joy, she said a silent prayer, hoping that the coldness around her husband's heart had thawed to forgive them.

"Good afternoon, Madam. Is Mr Adams Okal in?" the old man asked.

"Good afternoon, he is in. Welcome," she said as she shook their hands and ushered them into the sitting room.

Once they were seated, she offered them drinks and went in search of Adams. He was in the study room, working on his laptop. When she got in, he looked up, grinning.

"Are you very busy?" she asked, moving towards him.

"Not too busy for the most beautiful woman in the entire world," he said when she stopped right in front of him, appraising him with his eyes, sending a shiver down her body.

Adams Junior wiggled out of her arms, giggling and reaching out to his father, breaking their moment.

He winked at her, kissing her on the lips, and the kiss held so much promise in it. Later, she knew that he would make it up to her. She couldn't wait.

Adams took their son. They looked so much alike. The two most important men in her life.

"You have visitors." She touched his arm lightly.

"I wasn't expecting anyone. Who are they?" Confusion clouded his eyes, frown lines forming on his forehead.

"I don't know them." She shrugged nonchalantly.

"I guess we will find out then," he said, walking out of the room.

She followed him, her heart beating fast, and she wiped her hands on her dress.

***

When they got to the sitting room, Adams stood rooted to the ground, frozen. His long-lost family was on his turf, so unfamiliar and out of place. His old man slowly rose from his seat. Seth and Val looked at him expectantly. Akinyi fidgeted next to him, shifting her weight from one foot to another.

"My son, I am so glad to see you," the familiar voice of his father broke the silence.

How many times had Adams replayed and toyed with this reunion? After years of waiting, he had given up hope. But right here, right now, his family was here. He had mixed feelings—confusion, anger and relief all wrapped in one.

Adams turned to Akinyi, who was standing next to him. Her eyes were bright with hope, anticipation, and ever-present love for him. She reached for the baby, and he handed Junior over. She turned to leave.

"Please stay, my love." He tugged at her hand, needing her to anchor him. She nodded.

Adams walked to his father in three long strides. He gave his hand in greeting, but his father pulled him into a hug. His old man wrapped his arms around her neck, his eyes misting with tears.

When they pulled apart, Adams knew he had been deluding himself all this while. One couldn't run away from his roots. His brother Seth stood and embraced him. Next, he hugged Val, who had grown into a beautiful woman just as he had suspected.

Akinyi shook their hands a second time and sat next to Adams on the couch across from theirs. Adams looked at his father's greying and thinning hair. White hair was sticking out of his nose and ears, as was common with the old. He even had wrinkles on his face, and he was thinner. All these years, memories of his father had been of the same age he had left him in. His brother Seth was taller and even had a potbelly. He had matured.

"How have you been, my son?" The old man broke the silence.

"I have been fine. This is my wife, Lucy Akinyi, and that is my son, Adams Junior," he said.

His father nodded, pride in his eyes.

"Look, son, I am too old to hide behind a groundnut's farm. I am sorry for the way we treated you. It wasn't your fault that your mother died. We were bitter and wanted a scapegoat, and you were an easy target. We still love you, and you are welcome home anytime."

Adams knew his father to be an immensely proud man. This apology had taken all he had, and the earnest look in his eye told it all. Was it too late to apologize? Adams had been hurt to the point of numbness. He had wanted someone to believe him. But they had ganged up against him.

"But why did you accuse me of the death of mum? Why did it take you all this while to reach out to me?"

"I wish I had the answers to your questions. I know they will just be excuses. Please forgive us," his father pleaded, going down on his knees.

Adams shook his head, helping the old man to his feet. "No need for that, Baba."

"Please forgive us," Seth and Val pleaded further. Absolution and condemnation were both in his hands. He could forgive them and start on a clean slate or hold them accountable and lose them forever. Both fought for dominion within him. Long-held anguish still gushed deep inside him. He looked at them, wondering which way to go.

"Darling, please let it go," Akinyi whispered, pleading with her eyes, rubbing his back, soothing his frayed nerves.

He closed his eyes, the weight of bitterness and resentfulness, heavy like boulders, tearing the seams of his heart.

"I forgive you!" he blurted, afraid that if he didn't let out the words now, he'd never be able to sum up the courage.

Exhaling, all the hurt, the disappointment, the loneliness, the sadness expunged from his system with those three words. And he felt light. The weight that had sat heavily on him was finally put to rest. He found tears flowing down his cheeks, and his father went to embrace him. His siblings joined in. Akinyi looked on, beaming at him. They pulled apart, and it was like the old times. Seth started teasing him. They took turns in carrying the baby and getting to know Akinyi. They left in the evening, and Adams promised to visit them the following weekend.

***

After his family left, Adams excused himself and escaped to his study. Anguished cries echoed in the house. Akinyi paced outside the wooden door, her stomach knotting with dread. Knocking, it took a while before the door cracked open. He regarded her with sad bloodshot eyes, defeat slumping his shoulders. She closed the distance hugging him.

"Everything will work out, you'll see," she whispered, kissing him on the cheek.

He nodded. "Thank you. I'll be out in a few."

Walking away, Akinyi entered the kitchen and started preparing supper. She set the table as Adams joined them, his face bright though he was too quiet, and she wondered what was going through his head.

"Are you okay?" she asked, concern in her eyes.

"Yes, my love." He gave her a ghost of a smile.

They ate their meals in the companionable silence, Adams Junior nodding off. Akinyi breastfed before taking him to his bed.

When she came out, she found Adams had cleared their plates and was out seated on the porch. She paused at the door, taking in the night. The night air was cool, the scent of Moringa thick in the air. The sky was starry, with the half-moon shining bright. The crickets kept on their ceaseless chirping.

He looked up at her, the semi-darkness intensifying his eyes and features. God, he was handsome. He held out his hand, and she closed the distance, standing before him. He tapped his lap, and she sat on him, his musky scent making her thighs clench.

"What is on your mind?" She looked up at him.

"You," he said, pulling her closer, rubbing his nose on her neck, breathing her in.

She whimpered, her heart picking up speed.

"Is that so?" she whispered.

"Yes, that night you came out here after the burial of my friend Oti." His hands ran on her stomach, cupping her boobs.

"I remember. You were out here smoking." She tried to focus, but he wasn't making it easy.

"I was out here all alone. It was one of the lowest points in my life. I had been running for so long, but all my demons caught up with me on that night. Then you came to me." He stalled, looking up at the moon as if gathering his scattered thoughts.

"And?" She ventured, reining him in.

"I felt whole again. Like my life had gained some semblance of direction. Thank you."

"I love you with the whole of my heart and soul. You are the best husband and father."

He pulled her to straddle him, linking their forehead, his warm breath fanning her lips as their lips grazed. He dove in, kissing her fiercely, growling deep in his throat. She crushed her boobs on his chest, riding him through his trousers.

"Akinyi!" he croaked, his throbbing hard-on seeking her out.

He reached out between her legs and found her panty-less.

"Damn, woman!" Sinking his fingers into her warm, wet pussy.

She rode his finger, her mouth pouting as she threw her head back.

He lowered his trousers and entered her warmth, filling her. Then, with his wet open mouth on her neck, sucking, nibbling, his hands on her waist as she flew them to ecstasy. He took in her cries of pleasure as he gave an answering growl deep in his throat, spewing his seeds inside her.

She wanted it to last forever and beyond.

"Akinyi, I love you so much." Devouring her mouth with his. "I want to stay like this forever. Get lost in your tender warmth, never to be found."

The End

Thank you for reading A Small-Town Girl by Diana Anyango. If you enjoyed this story, please leave a review on the site of purchase.

If you want to know about exclusive discounts, special offers and competitions, sign up for our newsletter today!

Or simply visit:

https://www.loveafricapress.com/newsletter

OTHER BOOKS BY LOVE AFRICA PRESS

Inside Out by Emem Bassey

The Future King by Kiru Taye

The One That Got Away by Zee Monodee

Love In The Bar by Maggie Smart

CONNECT WITH US

Facebook.com/LoveAfricaPress

Twitter.com/LoveAfricaPress

Instagram.com/LoveAfricaPress

www.loveafricapress.com

CPSIA information can be obtained
at www.ICGtesting.com
Printed in the USA
LVHW010211150822
725929LV00004B/332